The New Cricut Design Space Guide 2021

A beginner's guide, updated, illustrated and detailed, follows you step by step in all operations with Cricut Machine.

TABLE OF CONTENT

INTRODUCTION

Cricut is the brand name for a range of scrapbooking home cutters (or cutters) and various projects produced by Provo Craft & Novelty, Inc. (also known as "Provo Craft"). from Spanish fork. Utah. The machines are used to cut paper, felt, vinyl, fabrics and other products such as fondant. Cricut is one of the many electronic cutting tools used by paper craftsmen, card makers, and scrap bookers.

Current models of Cricut are:

Cricut Maker

The Cricut Maker is used with Design Space, a cloud-based online software. It does not work alone. If you use Design Space on a desktop computer or laptop, an Internet connection is required. If you use the device with the Design Space app on an iOS device (iPad / iPhone), you can use the offline feature of this app to use the device and the Design Space without an Internet connection. Cricut Maker is an adaptable machine with interchangeable cutting and marking heads.

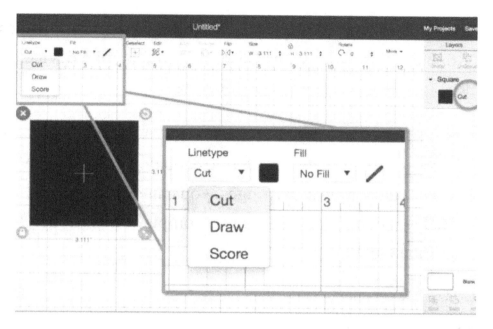

*Screenshot of the "Design Space 3" software **illustrated step by step**.*

Cricut Explore Air 2

A slight update of the air, it cuts twice as fast. Available in different colors and works with the current Space Design Space application.

Cricut Explore Air

This is a cordless machine that can cut tissue paper and more. It works with the current Space Design Space application.

Cricut Explore One

Outwardly similar to other Explore machines but has only one tool holder. You can cut and cut, but you have to do this in two steps.

Explore Cricut Maker

The Cricut Explore, Explore Air and Explore Air 2 systems each have a double tool holder for cutting and writing (or cutting and writing) in one step. Explore One has only one tool holder so it can cut and write (or cut and puncture) in 2 steps. Explore and Explore Air 2 has built-in Bluetooth.

However, for Explore One and Explorer, you'll need a Cricut Wireless Bluetooth Adapter to use with your iOS or Android mobile device, or to make wireless intersections from your computer

Cricut Expression 2

The Cricut Expression 2 was designed as a standalone machine. With the LCD touch screen and Cricut® cartridges, you can create projects without being connected to a computer. However, a computer was needed to update the firmware of the machine.

Cricut Expression

The Cricut Expression Machine had several fantastic features. Some favorites are automatic fill and bulk functions. You've been able to crop a multiple of the same image to quickly create a range of invitations, location settings, gifts, or other projects. There was a trick that could be used.

Cricut Mini

The Cricut Mini relied solely on Cricut Craft SPACE, a computer program that did not work anymore. The mini-circuit is outdated.

Cricut Imagine

Cricut Imagine machines use a special cutting mat with a white border and black registration marks, which is read by the machine before the printed images are precisely and accurately cut. The Imagine machine could not read other carpets.

Cricut Cake

Cricut Cake has been specially developed for cutting edible materials such as gum paste, glaze sheets, etc. As such, it has been constructed with food grade material. Every part of the machine that touches food was made of safe materials.

Create Cricut

The Cricut Create machine is designed to work with Cricut® cartridges as a stand-alone machine.

Cricut staff

The Cricut Personal V1 machine has been designed to work with original Cricut cartridges as a stand-alone machine.

Cricut Cuttlebug

The Cricut Cuttlebug machine is compatible with most popular die stamping and folding machines. B - cutters, A - plate spacers and C - plate adapters (sold separately) have different thicknesses so you can mix them.

BrightPad

Cricut BrightPad is available in mint green and rose gold. It is a modern light box that is very good for weeding, tracking, paper works, and jewelry making.

Gypsy Cricut

The Gypsy was a portable personalization device for Cricut® Personal, Create, Expression, Cake, Cake Mini, Expression 2 and Imagine. It allows you to store cartridge content, design with that content, and then connect to your Cricut machine to cut.

WHAT CAN I DO WITH CRICUT?

If you need something that is trimmed (or drawn or engraved or broken), Cricut is probably meant to be cut. Here are some project ideas:

Paper pennants for a party.

A leather bracelet

Iron vinyl for T-shirts.

Gift boxes and labels made of paper

Templates for wooden posters.

Vinyl sentences for coffee cups.

Felt Coasters

greeting

Custom bags

Water bottles with monogram

Paper flowers for bouquets.

Vinyl labels for your pantry.

color

Decals for model aircraft

CHAPTER 1: CRICUT

What is a Cricut machine?

Cricut Explore Air is a punching machine (also called a plotter or cutting machine). You can imagine it also as a printer Machine.

You create an image or design on your computer and send it to the computer. Apart from the fact that the Cricut computer does not print your design, but cuts it out of all material! Cricut Explore Air can cut paper, vinyl, fabric, hobby foam, glue paper, faux fur and much more!

If you want to use a Cricut as a printer, you can do that too! There is an accessory groove in the machine where you can load a marker and let Cricut "sketch" your design. It is perfect to have a nice look by hand if you do not write as well.

Cricut Explore One is the simplest and most economical machine that Cricut offers. With 199 US dollars, the price can not be exceeded. It has all the functions for cutting, writing and evaluating the Explore Air machines and can cut all materials (there are more than 100!). None of the three machines needs cartridges, although you can use your old cartridges altogether.

BUT it has two notable differences.

The first is that Bluetooth is not activated. This means that you must connect a cable from your device to your Cricut to connect the two. This is not a big problem, but it can be a little annoying depending on how your creation zone is set up.

The second is that there is no duplicate tool cartridge, so you can not write and cut (or score and cut) in the same pass.

You can still write and score; you just have to do it separately. Again, it is not a big pain if you do not write and write or write and cut a lot. If you cut alone, it does not matter much.

The simplest explanation is that Cricut Explore is an electronic cutting machine that looks like a printer. But instead of printing your designs on paper, use a very accurate knife and a set of rollers to cut almost anything you can imagine.

The Cricut series of cutting machines have been around for years. The first time I met Cricut, I thought it was just a machine for Scrapbooker. He cut out paper forms and fonts that were delivered in cartridges.

USES OF CRICUT

1. Vinyl stickers and stickers

You can do this with the Cricut Maker.

Vinyl can be cut quickly - all you have to do is create your design in Cricut Design Space and machine the machine with blades, weeds, and transfer the design to the desired surface.

2. Fabric cuts

One of numerous main selling points of the maker is that he is equipped with the brand new Rotary Blade. This means that the machine can cut almost any fabric.

We were always forced to use a special fabric cutter because the desktop slicers were simply not suitable for heavier fabrics. We love the fact that a maker is an all-in-one machine.

And it is also equipped with a textile cutting mat so that you can cut hundreds of fabrics without a carrier. Amazing!

3. Patterns

Another important pro of the maker is the huge library of sewing patterns that you can access after purchasing the machine.

It contains hundreds of patterns - including some of the Simplicity and Riley Blake designs - and means you can easily pick the pattern you want and the Maker will cut it for you.

4. Balsawood cuts

The Cricut Maker can cut up to 2.4mm thick material.

This means that thick fabrics that were previously unlimited in Cricut and Silhouette are now available. We can not wait to see wood!

5. Thick leather parts

For point 4, the maker can also cut thick leather!

6. Homemade cards

Papermakers are also not excluded with the Maker.

The performance and precision of the device make cutting paper and cards easier and faster than ever before. Your homemade cards have just gone up one level ...

7. Puzzles

With the knife blade, we know that the Cricut Maker can cut much thicker materials than ever before.

The first thing we want to try? Make our puzzle. We'll keep you up to date!

8. Christmas tree decorations

The Rotary Blade, which cuts every fabric, is the perfect tool for designing Christmas decorations.

Browse the sewing pattern library for Christmas patterns (we keep an eye out for gingerbread man's ornament!), Cut out the pattern with felt or other fabric, and sew it together.

9. Quilts

Cricut has teamed up with Riley Blake Designs to offer some patterned patterns in the library.

This means that you can use the maker to cut your quilts accurately before sewing them separately.

10. Felt dolls and stuffed animals

One of the Simplicity designs that we think of in the library with patterns is the pattern with felt dolls and clothes. We know a few little girls and boys who love a homemade doll to include in their collection.

Just pick the pattern, cut and sew. Easy!

11. Transfers of the T-shirt

Of course, the Cricut Maker is an expert in cutting out your heat transfer film to transfer your designs to textiles.

All you should do is design your transfer to Design Space, load the manufacturer's heat exchanger (or even use HTV glitter if you feel adventurous), start the machine with cutting, and then transfer iron on your T-shirt.

12. Baby clothes

Unfortunately, the Motricity of the Cricut Maker is only 12 "x 24", so you can not cut adult patterns on this machine.

However, this size should be just large enough to cut patterns for baby clothes.

13. Doll clothes

And doll clothes too!

14. Tissue applications

Also available separately is the blade glued in the housing, which allows you to design more complicated fabrics such as applications.

Unlike the rotating knife, the bound tissue sheet must be tied back on the material to cut effectively.

15. Calligraphy sign

The main selling point of Cricut Maker is the Adaptive Tool System.

This is the feature that keeps you, maker, forever. It is essentially a tooling system that not only fits with all Explore family tools and blades but also with all future Cricut tools and magazines.

16. Make jewelry

If you also want to make jewelry in addition to cutting jewelry, be sure to try combining both at the same time.

The strength of the Cricut Maker means you can cut thicker materials than before, which are well suited for intricate jewelry patterns.

17. Wedding cards and Save the Dates

We all know how 'low' spending, such as invitations and sexually transmitted diseases, can increase the mega costs of a wedding.

But as creators, we also know how to compensate for some of these costs by doing things yourself.

The Cricut Maker is perfect for beautiful invitations - you can not only cut out complicated paper designs, but also the calligraphy pen.

18 wedding menus, place cards, and favor markers

Of course, you are not limited to tinkering before the wedding, but you can also use your maker for the big day.

The air is the limit here, but it certainly starts with making menus, place cards and badges.

19. coloring book

Do you know these "mindful coloring books" that are currently in fashion? Well, if you do not feel like injecting the money for someone, why not make your own with the Cricut Maker?

All you need is paper, cardboard and a crackling design. And just tell the maker to make your unique coloring book with the Fine-Point pen.

20. Coasters

Another thing that we can expect with our brand new maker is coasters.

The world is your oyster when it comes to materials - from leather to quilts to metal plates to everything in between.

The sewing library also has some great checkout patterns to check out.

21. Fabric keychain

Another thing we noticed in the library with sewing patterns were some simple key designs for fabrics.

The Maker makes it easy again: cut out the pattern and sew it together.

22. Headbands and hair accessories

After Cricut has now been brought out a machine that can cut thick leather, we have a nice idea for complicated inspired by Steampunk her jewelry and even headbands.

Who would have thought that the Maker could be so useful for great fashion statements?

23. Cut open the Christmas tree

We know, we know ... everyone wants a real Christmas tree during the Christmas season.

In case you do not have SPACE for a towering tree in your living SPACE or, thank God, who is allergic to pine you are, you might want to create your tree.

Because the Cricut Maker is capable of cutting thick materials such as wood, we believe that an interlocking wood tree is a great project to experiment with this year.

No laser required if the maker is with you!

24. Cupcake toppers

Do you remember when Cricut launched the "Cake" slicer? It served to make molds of fondant, chewing gum and the like.

Well, the maker is not a specialized cake machine as the cake, but we think it is just the machine to make small and complicated paper products with which we can decorate our cake.

25. fridge magnets

Like the Cricut Explore machines, the Maker can remove magnetic material. Good news for magnetic collectors and those who want to chase their fridge!

26. Window stickers

Do you want to place an inspiring quote on your windows? Or maybe a cute little pattern on the rear window of your car?

With the Cricut Maker no problem, just load the machine with window clamps and make your design.

27. Scrapbooking ornaments

We are delighted to use our maker for decorations that we can use for scrapbooking.

While the Cricut machines have always been great at cutting complex designs, the wonderfully appealing new blades are the complexity of the past - even as cutting materials such as blotting paper.

28. Craft Foam Cuts

The Cricut machines have always been confirmed that they can cut artisan foam, but we have noticed that the result is never as perfect as we would like.

Not so with the Cricut maker: The force of 4 kg means that this machine can cut butter through Bastschaum and the View machines can be dusted.

29. Boxing and 3D shapes

The maker can not only handle all sewing patterns that you can throw but all old school newspapers that we know and love, including the ability to cut 3D shapes and boxes.

30. templates

If your goal with Maker is to create things that will help you do other beautiful things, then you're in luck.

This is the perfect template making machine - especially now when you can use thicker materials to lay out the templates, including wood.

31. Temporary tattoos

Fancy a tattoo, but not so enthusiastic about the commitment to life?

Do not worry; the manufacturer can engrave your design on tattoo paper - a transfer-coated paper - that you can use on your body.

32. Washi tape

Washi-Tape is the accessory of the year for Scrapbooker, but it can be surprisingly expensive to buy many craft shops.

So why not do it yourself? The Cricut Maker can cut out Washi Sheets so you can print and cut your designs.

33. Custom envelopes

When you're done with the handmade wedding invitations that we discussed earlier, you can continue with the envelopes.

However, it is not necessary to invest time and energy to handle them yourself if you have the manufacturer. With both a fine-point pen and a calligraphy pen, you can automatically address envelopes using the elegant font you want.

34. Glass Decals

One of our favorite experimental way with vinyl cutting is to cut designs for glassware. This is especially cool and effective when organizing theme parties.

For example, a summer barbecue and serving mojitos? Why do not you decorate mugs with palm stickers and coconuts?

To hold a Christmas party? Excellent - there is no better time than sticking the stickers with the holly and ivy on the egg cups!

35. Decorations

And just as you can do with most desktop cutting machines, the maker is certainly an excellent proof of how to make household decorations.

Whether beautiful billboards in your cabinets, beautiful cut-outs in your living SPACE or 3D wall hangings - you can do it with the Cricut Maker.

36. Pillow transfers

The quickest way to lighten a dull pillow or pillow is to add one of your home-made designs.

Many people use vinyl for heat transfer on their completely new maker machine to do just that. Our favorite vinyl version for pillows is the flocked, iron-on vinyl, which feels pleasantly textured.

37. 3D bouquet

Right - we are back on the subject of the wedding!

This is a distinct way to add a touch of homework to your wedding - or, even better, add flowers to your home without worrying about the impending death.

With intuitive tools such as the fine-point sheet and pen, the Maker is well-prepared for complex paper crafting techniques.

You have in a short time a beautiful, immortal bouquet!

38. Gift Cards

Gift cards are one of the annoying topics that grow quickly over time - especially during the holiday season.

But with a Cricut you will never have to buy these labels again - just make it yourself! Just add cards.

39. purses and handbags

With this unbelievable range of patterns, you can use the Maker to create a whole range of purses, purses and even handbags.

Here it is probably useful to buy the knife to cut through the thick leather

40. Peter Pan collars

We said baby and doll clothes are about the size of the clothing patterns you can cut in Cricut Maker.

Well, that was a lie, sorry! - you can certainly cut patterns for adult clothing accessories here.

41. Cover for the Cricut Maker

We do Meta - you can also use the Maker to do things for the Maker. A dust cover for example - we love that the maker can cut canvas!

42. Game cushion

This is for the sewers.

We've seen at least eight funky pillow patterns with name patterns in the library - if you're not inspired to sew hand in hand, we're not sure what it's going to do!

43. Pillows and pillows

With the Maker, you can also cut patterns for small pillows and pillows.

These are small since the maximum size is only 12 "x 24", but that's enough for decorative pillows for the living SPACE and the nursery.

43. Pillows and Cushions

With the Maker, you can also cut patterns for small cushions and pillows.

These sizes will be quite small because the maximum cut-off size is only 12 x 24 inches, but that is sufficient for decorative cushions for the living SPACE and the nursery.

44. Dog clothes

If you have a toy or a small dog, you can also make some exciting things with the Maker.

At the moment this is limited to accessories - especially hats. We know that our dogs would not sit on their heads for two seconds, but it could work for you if your dog likes a good photo session!

45. socks

Of course, it is summer at the time of writing, but autumn and winter are just around the corner.

Make sure your tootsies do not miss the crafting by cutting a few woolly sock patterns on the Cricut Maker. They look like they are a piece of cake to sew together too!

46. Art on the wall

We've talked a lot about the paperwork you can do with the maker, but we think it's worth noting that wall art is also an option for you.

The precision that the Maker offers is so advanced that you can easily make something beautiful and perfect. No slipping and tearing parts of your design!

47. Hanging notice board

The Maker can cut cork leaves so that you have enough possibilities to make your own unique wall organization board.

48. cupcake holder

We have said before that you could use the Cricut Maker to make cupcake toppers, but what is the cake below?

If you make your cupcake holders, you can create general, simple thin paper holders that are scored with the score pen. Or you can become very creative and make your cupcakes in the style of Alice in Wonderland for your cupcakes.

Reasons You Need a Cricut Maker in Your Life

1. The Cricut Maker cuts the fabric

Whether you are a beginner or a beginner in sewing, that's a very big deal.

The Cricut machine can cut the fabric. The fabric must first be glued to another element to get thicker and thicker, such as with Heat N 'Bond or a similar product.

However, with the Cricut Maker, you can lay the fabric alone on the new pink carpet. He is ready to cut!

The Cricut Maker can also cut all kinds of fabrics: silk, organza, cotton, denim, felt and leather!

All this is made possible by the new Cricut rotary knife, which slides smoothly over the fabric and cuts perfectly.

2. New digital pattern library for Cricut Maker Machine

Now you can access hundreds of ready-made seam templates from Simplicity, Riley Blake and more! Just pick a project that you like, and the manufacturer Cricut will cut it for you. You do not need hours to cut patterns and fabrics - let the manufacturer do all the work so you can do the part you love - sewing!

It's also a great way to introduce children to sewing. With almost no preparatory work children can learn how to sew quickly and efficiently!

3. The Cricut Maker can cut heavy materials

Not when sewing? Do not worry, Cricut Maker can do many other things!

It can cut heavier materials than any Cricut machine — Balsa wood, birch, matte boards, billboards, cork, thick leather, etc. With the new knife blade (coming soon) you can cut thicker surfaces up to 3/32 ", opening up a whole new world of creative possibilities, right ?!

Thanks to the knife blade, you can do everything from puzzles to wooden models, etc. I already have a list of everything I will do as soon as this blade is available in the next few months!

4. The new Cricut machine is a beauty

Is not It may sound stupid, but if I keep a machine on my desk all the time, I want it to be beautiful.

The Cricut Maker is designed to be beautiful and does not have to be stowed. She is elegant, supple and has a lot of thinking.

The designers and engineers of Cricut were so smart when creating Cricut Maker! You've created a docking location where you can place your phone or tablet while you work. They even added a USB charging port, which is great there is SPACE for your tools and equipment on the left and rear of the machine, so you'll always have your needs where you need them.

5. New design area updated with new features

The design SPACE, where you design and build projects for your Cricut machines, offers exciting new features. Now you can work offline on a project so that you can work on an airplane and wait for children to queue or if there is no Wi-Fi connection available. Goal!

SnapMat is another nice feature. With SnapMat, you can take a photo of your material on the cutting mat to know exactly where your image is being cut. Brilliant. Not only does this help you place your image exactly where you want it, but also to use paper and fabric with less waste.

6. More tools than ever before and more (including the turning tool)!

One of the really interesting aspects of Cricut Maker is all the tools available to help you create and create in some ways.

The fine point, the deep point, the knife blade, the rotating blade, the fine pen, the washable fabric pen, the calligraphy pen, and the marker are amazing tools that you can use to craft in ways you would never have thought possible!

What is amazing is that the Cricut Maker grows with you. Cricut is creating more and more tools associated with Cricut Maker to add tools to your crafting capabilities.

Maintenance of Cricut machines

Cleaning the Cricut machines

• Carefully wipe the exterior walls with a damp cloth.

• Immediately wipe off excess moisture with leatherette or other soft cloth.

• Do not use chemical or alcoholic cleaning products (including but not limited to acetone, benzene, and carbon tetrachloride) on the machine. Abrasives and cleaning agents must also be avoided. Do not immerse the device or parts of it in water.

• Stay away from food and liquids and do not try to eat or drink during operation.

• Store dry and dust-free.

• Avoid excessive heat or cold. Do not leave the machine in the car, where excessive heat can melt or damage plastic parts.

• Do not expose it to direct sunlight for extended periods.

Take care of the cutting mat.

• Expect the Cricut Cutting Mat to be used between 25-40 full-mesh cuts before it needs to be replaced.

• The actual life of the cutting mat depends on the settings used and the paper types cut.

• If your paper no longer adheres to the cutting mat, you must replace the mat.

• It is always recommended to use only the original Cricut replacement.

You can replace Cricut machines with parts from Cricut itself. You can also get parts from many other places online.

CHAPTER 2: CRICUT MODELS

Cricut Machines simplifies all projects and tasks related to cutting, tracking and precision manufacturing. Cricut Machines gives you the freedom to create any kind of project, from paper craft to vinyl decals. Simply connect your tablet, smartphone or computer to a Cricut computer to get your project up and to run.

There are various Cricut models to choose from. If you're considering buying a Cricut for your home or business, let this comparison of Cricut machines help you.

We will explain the features, advantages, and disadvantages of using any type of Cricut and hope that in the end, you will find the machine that best suits your needs and budget.

A list of comparisons of Cricut machines and reviews:

1. Cricut maker

- Supplied with extendable tools

- You can use different models

- Use a computer or a mobile device

2. Cricut Explore Air 2

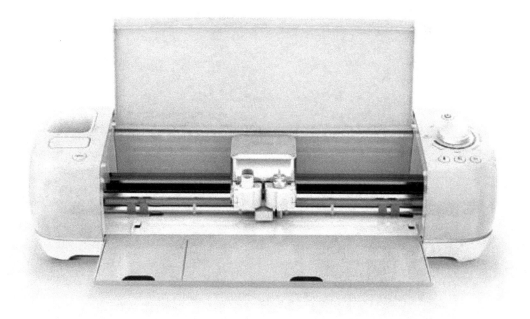

- Cuts with the highest precision

- Over 370 fonts written

- Cut and write twice faster

3. Cricut Explore Air

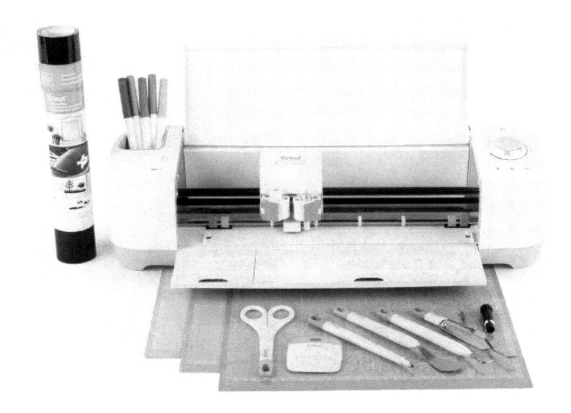

- You can work wirelessly

- Cut and write, cut and mark

- Works with Cricut cartridges

4. Cricut Explore 1

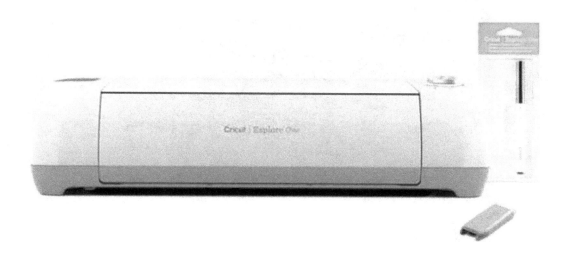

- With more than 50,000 images and fonts

- Upload your pictures for free

- Quickly print and cut

5. Cricut Expression 2

- Practical LCD touch screen

- Access to the craft SPACE Cricut

- With preloaded Cricut cartridges

- Works with all types of materials

6. Cricut Expression one

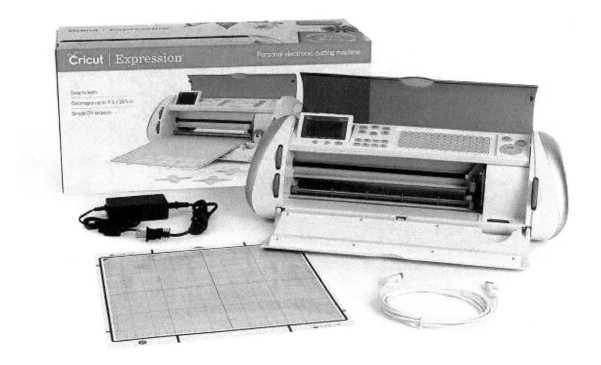

- With six modes and four functions

- With a portable design

- Works with the craft SPACE Cricut

7. Cricut Mini

- Comes with a free online application

- Cut many materials

- Simple and easy to use

1. Cricut maker

Cricut Maker Review

You can do it all with the Cricut Maker. This is the flagship of Cricut and can be used with almost any type of material, from balsa wood to paper. Cricut Maker has an expandable toolset: it comes with a blade, pen and marking tool. By using the rotating blade supplied with the Cricut Maker, you can cut any fabric as quickly and accurately as possible. With the knife blade of the machine, you can make very deep cuts in thicker and heavier materials like balsa and cardboard. You can also choose from hundreds of digital models in the Cricut database. The machine can easily cut and mark all these parts, and you just have to complete your project. Cricut Maker simplifies sewing and quilting. You also have the right to use your designs. Just download it and use it with the Cricut app.

This Cricut model is one of the most popular models but has some disadvantages. The knife blade, with which you can also cut thick material, is available separately. Not all pictures are free from their picture library, and in fact, you have to pay for the best ones. Some complain that it takes time to work with an iPad. Consider these disadvantages before purchasing the Cricut Maker.

Specifications

-With extendable tools: rotating blade, knife blade, and pins

-The rotating blade can cut quickly and accurately

-The knife blade is suitable for thin and thick materials

-With fine tip, 12 x 12-inch cutting mat

-Comes with hundreds of digital sewing patterns

-With a simple design application; Upload projects to a computer or mobile device

-You can use your drawings

-With a device docking slot

-With wireless Bluetooth technology

-With a USB port to charge the used device

Advantages

Allows the processing of various materials

Supplied with extendible tools

You can use other models from your database

Use your computer or mobile device with the Cricut

With Device Dock you can work closely with the device

The disadvantages

The knife blade is sold separately

Complaints that it does not work with an iPad

2. Cricut Explore Air 2

You can do a lot with a personal cutter, custom vinyl stickers for the interior design. With the Cricut Explore Air 2, you can download our templates, or you can use any template from their huge library of predefined templates. You can create your designs on a PC, tablet, laptop or mobile phone and easily import them into Cricut Design Space. The Design Space app can be used for both Android devices and iOS devices. With Cricut Explore Air 2 you can use more than 100 materials for different projects with the Smart Set Dial. This device can connect to your PC or device and also works via Bluetooth to cut wireless documents.

The use of Cricut Explore Air 2 for Android was straightforward, but some users using iOS have difficulty using Design Space. If you're using an iPad or products with the iOS system, consider using a Cricut model that works well with your device.

Specifications

Cut complex details with the utmost precision

With Cricut Pens, you create "handwritten" cards and other projects

With over 370 fonts to choose from

With Scoring Stylus, you can fold cards, boxes, envelopes, acetate and create 3D paper objects

With the fast mode for a cut twice as fast

You can work with more than 100 types of materials

Use Design Space to work with files from any device

Can work with an Android or iOS device

Wireless cut with Bluetooth

With the Cricut Image Library

Advantages

Cutting with the highest precision

Write over 370 fonts

Scoring stylus folds lines for different projects

Cut and write twice faster

Works with more than 100 materials

Design with Design Space everywhere

Connection to devices via Bluetooth

The disadvantages

Problems with the design SPACE

Offline Design Area is available for iOS users only

3. Cricut Explore Air

You can work on wireless projects using Cricut Explore Air. This cutting machine has a Bluetooth wireless feature that allows you to work with your tablet, smartphone or iPad. It has double carriages so you can cut, write or mark in one step. You can even download your free pictures at Cricut Design Space. This device supports almost all design files. Working on different materials? You can cut more than 60 types of materials easily and accurately, so you do not waste expensive materials like leather. The Smart Set Wheel lets you make simple adjustments to work like a pro, even if you're using Cricut Explore Air for the first time. You can work with your templates, use Cricut cartridges, or use templates from the extensive library collection.

Cricut Explore Air is very easy to use, but its long-term use can be expensive if you do not intend to use your designs. Fonts and images start at $ 0.90, which can be expensive if you want to print more patterns. Downloading your drawings is free.

Specifications

With integrated Bluetooth for wireless work

With double cartridge for simultaneous cutting, writing or marking

Compatible with .svg, .jpg, .png, .bmp, .gif and .dxf files

Cuts more than 60 different materials

Works with all Cricut cartridges

With integrated memory components

Advantages

You can work wirelessly

Cut and write, cut and score at the same time

You can use your images or use any image from a huge library

Store pens, knives, and other accessories in storage compartments

Works with Cricut cartridges

The disadvantages

You have to buy additional tools and accessories

You have to buy drawings and fonts

4. Cricut Explore One

With Cricut Explore One, you can create projects and cut different types of materials. This cutting tool uses a wireless Bluetooth adapter, so you can use any Bluetooth-enabled device to create beautiful projects. You can also download your creations and images for free and cut them easily. The Cricut Explore One can cut seamlessly from paper to vinyl to cardboard to leather at any time. If you do not have any patterns, you can also choose over 50,000 Cricut images in the image library. You can even use old Cricut cartridges.

Cricut Explore is very handy because you can cut and trace wirelessly. However, this device does not have built-in wireless capabilities. You must purchase a wireless Bluetooth adapter separately to use this feature. This is associated with additional costs for the users. You will also need to pay more for using fonts and images in the image library, which will incur additional costs.

Specifications

Download your creations for free or choose one from the Cricut Image Library.

Use the Cricut Design Space for PC, Mac, iPad or iPhone

Works wirelessly by adding a wireless Bluetooth adapter

Work on different materials, from thin paper to thick vinyl

Use the fonts installed by your PC

Compatible with .svg, .jpg, .bmp, .gif, .png and .dxf files

Works with Cricut cartridges

With a practical tool and accessory holder

You need not to make any adjustments with the Smart Set wheel or make your settings

Create projects in minutes

Advantages

Works wirelessly with a Bluetooth adapter

With more than 50,000 images and fonts in the Cricut Image Library

Upload your free pictures and designs

Design with your device or PC with Design Space

No adjustment is required with the Smart Set Wheel

Quickly print and cut

The disadvantages

Bluetooth adapter sold separately

The use of pictures costs from 0.99€

5. Cricut Expression 2

You can use your computer or device, or use the practical Cricut Expression 2 LCD touchscreen, a brand new design that lets you take the project wherever you go. Cut out fonts and pictures and use your computer. Own designs. Cricut Expression 2 also works with Cricut cartridges so you can use the old cartridges of your other Cricut models. You can conveniently control the machine via the touchscreen LCD screen and also work with all kinds of materials.

With Expression 2, you can manage your projects from the LCD screen. You can change print and speed settings, or customize your settings for specific types of media. You can use thin materials such as tissue, paper or aluminum foil or thick materials such as vinyl, chipboard or cardboard. It has three pre-installed Cricut cartridges with fonts, phrases, and pictures. You will need to purchase additional Cricut cartridges for more fonts and images.

Specifications

With color LCD touch screen

Compatible with Cricut cartridges

The contents of the Cricut cartridge are preinstalled in the device

Connects to the free Cricut Craft SPACE design software

Other image editing features such as size, rotation, and vertical/horizontal tilt

Three types of preloaded fonts, 40 phrases, and 110 pre-loaded overlay images

With Cricut Essentials cartridge and alphabet cartridge

Works with all types and sizes of materials

Uses a 12 "x 24" cutting mat (sold separately)

With additional features such as auto-fill, number and page customization

Use a computer to design and cut the Cricut Craft SPACE

Use images from the Cricut Image Library

Advantages

Thanks to the practical LCD touch screen, you can work without having to connect to a PC

Preview images with an LCD screen

Access to the craft SPACE Cricut

Adjust the pressure and speed with the LCD screen

With preloaded Cricut cartridges

Works with all types of materials

Maximize the use of materials with Fit to Page

The disadvantages

You have to pay more to buy more Cricut cartridges

You must pay more to use the fonts and images in the Cricut Image Library.

6. Cricut Expression 1

With Cricut Expression 1 you can make further adjustments for different projects. This electronic cutting machine works in conjunction with Cricut Craft SPACE, where you can edit drawings and improve your output. With six modes and four functions, you can create different projects. You can also use fast cutting and trailing speeds, which makes projects faster, ideal for professional use. Expression 1 is also portable. You can take it anywhere. At school, home or in the office. It has an LCD screen but does not touch. Your purchase comes with a 12 "x 12" cutting mat, so you do not have to buy them.

Cricut Expression 1 is portable and works effectively. You can create many types of projects, but you need to buy cassettes because they are not

provided. Technically, you can not build a project before it comes out of the box.

Specifications

Works with the craft SPACE Cricut

With six modes and four different customization features

Can cut images to the minute 0.25 " in 23.5 "

With normal LCD screen

Portable design

Purchase delivered with a 12 "x 12" cutting mat

Cut quickly and efficiently

Advantages

With six modes and four functions

Fully customizable to create better designs

With a portable design

Comes with a 12 " x 12 " cutting mat

Works with Cricut Craft SPACE

The disadvantages

The delivery does not include a cartridge

Problems with the sticky mat

Not compatible with other cartridges

7. Cricut Mini

You will appreciate the Cricut Mini, which despite its small size can cut up to 8.5 inches of material as well as shapes and fonts from 1/4 "to 11.5". You always get precise cuts. With the name you know it's portable and lightweight, and you can take it anywhere. You need a laptop or computer connected to the Internet to use Cricut Mini to connect to Gypsy. This model Cricut is for you, if you want to save space or if you need a machine, you can switch from one place to another.

Specifications

Can cut up to 8.5 "x 12"

Can cut shapes and fonts from 1/4 " to 11.5 "

Must be connected to a laptop or computer to run Cricut Gypsy

Works with the free online design software Cricut Craft SPACE

You can use many images from the Cricut Image Library.

Edit drawings with size, tilt, rotation, or inverse functions

Can work with all types of the materials, from thick vinyl to thin, delicate films

Small and portable

Low weight

Quiet to use

Comes with four sheets of free card paper 8.5 " x 11 "

Advantages

Comes with a free online application, Cricut Craft SPACE

Edit your work by resizing, tilting, rotating, and mirroring

Cut a variety of materials like chipboard, vinyl, and films

Simple and easy to use

Comes with an 8.5 "x 12" Cricut cutting mat

The disadvantages

You need a laptop or PC to work

Comparison of all Cricut machines

1. Cricut Maker vs. Explore Air 2

The main difference between the Cricut Maker and the Explore Air 2 is that the manufacturer has a knife blade that allows you to cut thicker and harder materials such as leather, balsa, and chipboard. The manufacturer is also heavier because he should exert a higher pressure when using the knife blade. Of course, Explore Air 2 can also cut thick material, but the manufacturer makes it faster and more accurate with the knife blade.

The manufacturer can cut colored paper and patterned paper with its new improved sensor, while the Air 2 cuts only white paper. The Air 2 has a

Smart Set dial that allows you to select the material to use. It seems that it only works with a few materials compared to the Cricut Maker, which can very quickly and easily cut very thin to thick materials.

The Cricut Maker has a more elegant design with some metal elements. It also has several compartments for storing accessories such as scissors, blades, pens, and markers, as well as a holder for tablets or devices. Air 2 has only one compartment for tools and accessories.

In short, if you're looking for a Cricut that can cut deeper and faster, handle more types of material, and have more SPACE for accessories, the Cricut Maker is for you. The Cricut Maker is the most expensive Cricut model as a flagship cutting machine. However, if you only work on basic projects and want to take your Cricut with you, the Explore Air 2 model may be better for you.

2. Explore Air 2 vs Explore Air

The Explore Air and Explore Air 2 Cricut models are two of the most popular models in the Explore range. Although these two cutting machines belong to the same Explore family, there are important differences that you need to consider before choosing the right machine for your needs. Both Explore Air 2 and Air 2 have the Smart Set switch, which lets you tune the machine to the material you want to cut. Both devices are Bluetooth

enabled so you can work wirelessly. Both work with Cricut cartridges or you can use images and fonts from the image library. Both machines have no rotating fabric blade, no knife blade, and no adaptive tooling system.

The main difference between Explore Air and Explore Air 2 is that the Air 2 has Fast mode to cut and write up to 2x faster than the Air. Air is available in Blue, Turquoise, Gold, and Wild while Air 2 is available in Mint, Blue, Pink, Anna Griffin, and Lilac. If you're searching for a faster, more efficient product line of Cricut Explore devices, the Explore Air 2 is better for your needs. But if you do not mind the speed and you do not want to pay more, you can settle for Explore Air.

3 Explore Air vs. Explore One

The Cricut Explore Air and Explore One model are two lightweight and easy-to-carry Cricut models. You can take them anywhere to work: at home, at school or in the office. Both models are equipped with the Smart Set dial, so you can easily configure the device and work with specific types of material. Both Explore models can cut a variety of materials from fine paper to heavy leather and vinyl. Both models can always be connected to a PC, a Mac and iOS mobile devices. However, Explore One does not have built-in Bluetooth for wireless cutting. You must purchase a Cricut

Bluetooth adapter to allow the device to run wirelessly. Explore One has an accessory adapter that you must purchase separately. With this adapter, you can attach the one-pen adapter to write with your Explore One.

Between Air Explorer and Explore One, Air is the more convenient choice if you are looking for a Cricut machine that is ready for wireless communication. It also has a double tool holder for cutting and writing, so you do not have to buy a tool adapter. Save time and money by buying accessories and upgrades with Explore One with Explore Air.

4. Explore Air vs. Explore Air Gold

Well, comparing Explore Air and Explorer Air Gold, which Cricut is the best and which will work for you? There is no difference between the Air and Gold specifications. Both devices have the Smart Set dial to define the type of material you will use with Cricut. Both are Bluetooth to enable wireless cutting and writing, and both feature a double tool holder to simplify cutting and to write the Cricut.

With both machines, you will be able to cut a variety of materials and upload your images for free with the Design Space application. You can use Cricut cassettes on both machines. You can also connect your PC, iOS device, or Mac devices to Explore Air Gold and Air. The only difference is the actual design. The Air Gold has a gold band surrounding the lower body of the machine. This makes the Air Gold more elegant and undoubtedly more expensive than the Explore Air model.

Explore Air Gold is perfect for the office and a great home cutting tool. If you are the most people who are excited about the beauty of the Air Gold brand, do not pay anything. However, if you value design, Explore Air is a better choice for you.

5. Explore 1 vs. an expression 2

If you just look at the design of Explore One and Expression 2, you will notice something very different. Expression 2 has a mini-touchscreen that houses the machine's main control panel. You can modify your design very well and improve the speed and pressure on the material you want to cut using the LCD touchscreen. The Explore One LCD is missing, but it can be controlled by a PC or device if it has a Bluetooth adapter. Both machines can cut different materials and work with Cricut cartridges.

Compared to Expression 1, Expression 2 is a complete improvement. Removed the physical buttons whose screen is completely touch-triggered. In terms of design and specifications, Expression 2 outperforms Explore One and its predecessor. The LCD touchscreen and wireless connectivity will seduce you. It's harder than the Explore One, but its features and design make it a winner.

6. Expression 1 vs. Cricut Mini

If you want to use and buy a Cricut, but this is not too expensive, the Cricut Mini may be the best choice for you. This slicer is a lighter version of traditional Cricut models. It can cut and write 8.5 "x 12" paper and make smaller than larger cuts. It can work with a variety of materials, is lightweight and easy to carry. It only costs a fraction of the usual Cricut models, but is this cheaper alternative to Cricut the better choice if you need to work on larger and more complex projects?

Let's take a look at the Mini vs. Expression 1, one of the most popular Cricut models on the market. The Mini can print on plain paper and cut and write on most media. However, it must be connected to a PC or laptop connected to the Internet. The mini is lightweight, but you always have to have a laptop with you when working remotely.

Expression 1 has an LCD screen and buttons that let you change your design when using the device. You do not need a computer or laptop. Expression 1 comes with a SchoolBook Plantin font and cartridge. You can adjust the printout and speed of Printout 1 via the LCD screen. You can also use six cutting modes and four functions, so you can easily select the ideal setting for your cutting or tracing requirements.

Expression 1 is significantly heavier than the Cricut Mini. So if you need a small, compact cutting machine that you can take anywhere, consider the

Mini Cricut. However, if you want a more efficient and faster-cutting tool, Expression 1 is the cutting tool that best suits your needs.

CHAPTER 3: MATERIALS THAN CAN BE WOORKED ON USING CRICUT MACHINE

What Materials Can A Cricut Machine Cut?

Many people think that a Cricut machine is only for cutting paper or vinyl, but it can do much more! A Cricut Explore machine can cut more than 100 different materials, and the new Cricut Maker has a rotating blade and a deep knife blade that can cut even more. Below is the list of what the Cricut machine can work on:

Cardboard and paper

The Cricut is great for cutting paper and cardboard, but it's not just about cutting scrapbook paper! Discover all paper types that a Cricut machine can cut:

adhesive cardboard

carton

cereal box

building paper

copy paper

Flat cardboard

Flocked cardboard

Flocked paper

Embossed paper

A sheet of black board

Freezer paper

Glitter cardboard

glitter paper

Power board

Kraft paper

Metal card stock

Metallic Paper

Billboard made of metal

Notebook paper

paper bags

parchment

carton

beaded board

Pearly paper

photos

Photo Frame mat

Be post

bulletin board

rice paper

Scrapbook paper

Shimmering paper

Fixed maps

Watercolor paper

waxed paper

White cardboard

vinyl

Vinyl is another great material that can cut the Cricut machine. Vinyl is great for signs, decals, stencils, graphics, etc.

Adhesive vinyl

Vinyl table

Wipe off vinyl dry

Glitter vinyl

Shiny vinyl

Holographic vinyl

Matt vinyl

Metal vinyl

Vinyl outdoors

Printable vinyl

vinyl mask

Iron on

Iron on vinyl, also known as Thermal Transfer Vinyl, is one of my favorite materials for cutting with my Cricut! You can use iron-on vinyl to decorate t-shirts, tote bags or other fabric items.

Flocked iron on

Iron sheet on

Iron shimmering

Shiny iron on

Glittering holographic iron

Iron on Matt

iron on

Neon iron on

Printable iron

Fabrics and textiles

The Cricut cuts fabrics perfectly, but you certainly want to use a stabilizer like Wonder Under or Heat's Bond before cutting. These fabrics and fabrics can be cut with a Cricut Explore machine, but you can cut even more with the rotating blade of a Cricut Maker machine.

sacking

canvas

cotton

denim

Duck fabric

leatherette

Wrong suede

feeling

flannel

leather

linen

Metallic leather

oilskin

polyester

Printable fabric

silk

Felt

Other materials

In addition to fabric, paper, and vinyl, Cricut can also cut tons of other specialty materials. Here are some funny ideas!

adhesive film

Glue wood

aluminum foil

aluminum foil

balsawood

Birch wood

Cork board

corrugated cardboard

Artisanal mousse

duct tape

Embossable sheet

acetate sheet

sparkling wine

Magnetic leaves

Metallic parchment

paint chips

Plastic packaging

Printable magnetic foils

Printable sticker paper

Retractable plastic

Can of soda

stencil material

tissue

Temporary tattoo paper

Transparency film

parchment

Washi leaves

Washi tape

Window is clinging

wood paint

gift wrap

Cricut Maker

The Cricut Maker machine has ten times the cutting capacity of the Explore machines, as well as a rotating blade and a knife blade that can cut even more material. The Cricut Maker can cut materials up to 2.4mm thick and more than 125 types of fabrics, including:

chiffon

cashmere

fleece

jersey

jute

knitwear

taupe

muslin

seersucker

dishcloth

tulle

tweed

velvet

CHAPTER 4: TOOLS AND ACCESSORIES OF CRICUT

Cricut Tools

weeding tool

Cricut Wedding Toolset

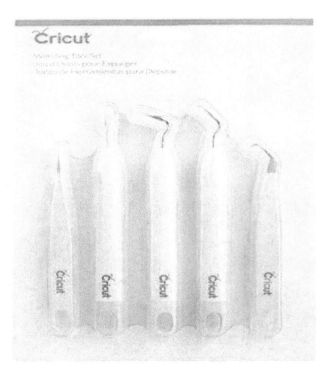

If there is one very important tool you want, it is a weed control tool. Although the spatula and tweezers are good, the weeding tool is necessary to lift the vinyl.

There are many different tools people use to weed, and they all work to make the vinyl stand out.

Cricut Wedding Tool is the most popular tool, but I recommend the Weeder Toolset because it contains finer points

Some other popular tools for weeding are:

Ballpoint Pen - This tool is great for smaller parts and lets you burst vinyl bubbles without cracking. Although it is comfortable and precise, it is not curved to hold the vinyl peeled off.

Dentist Choice - Users who use dental tips for weeding swear by them. They are good, but the handles may not be so comfortable.

Exacto Knife - The tip is small and precise enough to fit in the smallest details. Combine this with tweezers so as not to damage the project.

Experiment with different types and find out which weed tools are best for you.

Scraper

Cricut XL scraper

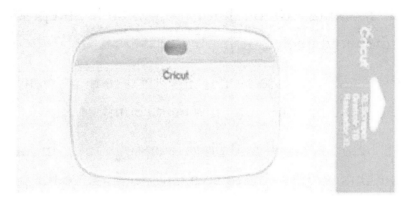

Clean carpet is important for clean cuts and to ensure that your material does not move during cutting. The spatula can help to remove tiny parts, but the squeegee does the job much faster. It is also useful to remove all bubbles out of the vinyl.

Spatula

Spatula Cricut: The spatula is another indispensable tool. When you lift material off the cutting mat, you do not want to worry about the cutting mat being torn off. The spatula ensures that the mat material is raised simply. The spatula is also used with the scraper to keep the carpet clean and free of debris. Cricut sells the spatula and scrapes together at a reasonable price. There is no reason not to have her!

Tweezers

Cricut Tweezers

If you do not have tweezers yet, they are very useful. I like to wear two different types, one for vinyl and the other for picking up tiny objects.

Well, it's not a Cricut tool, but it's too good not to share it! The tweezers I prefer for weeding are the Pazzles Needle Point tweezers. These braces have a pointed tip, making them great for vinyl. These points are good enough to pick up the vinyl directly from the center without having to use the edges. They can take even the smallest cases!

The other tweezers I like are mainly used to pick up objects and hold them in place. Cricut clips are no longer sold separately. If you're always looking for a good pair, the craft tweezers from EK Tools are strong! They are perfect for picking up rhinestones and other ornaments by doing the reverse. The opposite action is great not to hurt one's hands.

Scissors

Cricut scissors

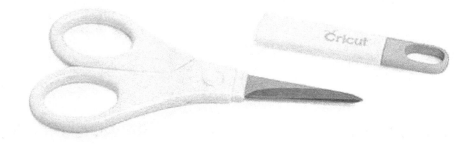

Good scissors can make a difference. The Cricut scissors are made of hardened stainless steel blades that produce even cuts while remaining durable. The pair of scissors is quite sharp and comes with a micro-tip blade. Working with the smallest details in smaller areas is, therefore, easier and cleaner down to the smallest point. It also has a colored and replaceable protective tip that keeps the scissors secure.

Paper cutter

Cricut Craft Knife

A router is very handy if you just want to make cuts — no need to use a
ruler and scissors. A paper cutter makes cutting easier, especially when
working with vinyl. Cricut has its paper cutter, but the slightly more
advanced one is the Fiskars SureCut paper cutter. He even has the
opportunity to score points to achieve those perfect wrinkles.

Brayer

Cricut Brayer

If you work with a larger fabric or vinyl (or something really), you want a brayer. Not completely stabilizing the material before cutting is one of the most common mistakes beginners make. A repair operation solves this problem by sticking the material to the Cricut mat without damaging it.

Extra Mat

Cricut Mat Variety Pack

Something you should also have a backup of is mats. There's nothing annoying when you're in the middle of the project and find your carpets are no longer sticking. There are ways to rebuild your cutting mat to save money, but it's always a good idea to have more carpets.

You need extra carpets for the most common types of carpet. Make sure you get mats for the right material:

LightGrip (blue) - for paper and board projects

Standard Grip (Green) - for vinyl and iron

StrongGrip (Purple) - for cardboard, thick cardboard and other thicker materials

FabricGrip (Pink) - for the fabric

Cricut EasyPress

Cricut EasyPress 2 reviews

If you're still using iron for heat transfer vinyl, it's time for an upgrade. The Cricut EasyPress makes things much easier than an iron. No peeling after 1 or 2 erosions. The EasyPress eliminates all uncertainties in terms of good weather and the right temperature.

If you have SPACE, you can get a real hot press for a little more money. Consider a hot press for beginners, especially if you are doing something in bulk or for commercial purposes.

BrightPad

Cricut Bright Pad

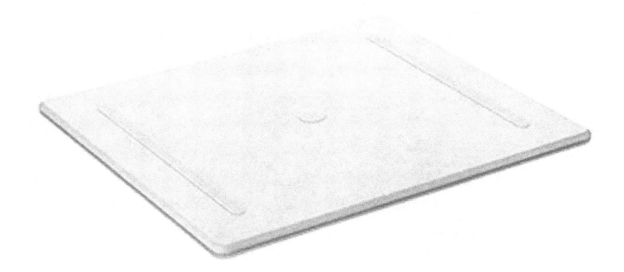

BrightPad is ideal for many reasons. First, it is much easier to visualize the cutting lines. If you have more than just a cup, this will help you a lot. You can even use it to draw and customize patterns.

Set of essential tools

Cricut Essential Tool Kit, Many of these tools, can be purchased in batches to save you money. The Cricut Essential Tool Set contains everything you need to get started - perfect for beginners!

This kit includes:

Tweezers for lifting and securing sensitive materials

Weeder, to remove small negative cuts

Scissors with blade protection

Spatula for lifting carpet cuts

Scraper to polish the material and clean all cutting mats

Scoring stylus to add fold lines to cards and envelopes

High-quality mower for materials up to 12 "wide

Replacement blade for the mower

The scoring blade lets you add score lines to your projects

CHAPTER 5: USE AND CONFIGURATION OF CRICUT *DESIGN SPACE* SOFTWARE

Design space

Cricut Design Space is an app that lets you design and cut wirelessly with Cricut Explore and Cricut Maker machines. Create a whole new project or browse thousands of images, ready-made Make It Now projects and fonts in the Cricut® Image Library. The app is cloud-based and synced across all your devices, so you can open your projects and images when you're inspired. Use your built-in camera to visualize your project against a realistic background. Then connect wirelessly to your Cricut Explore or Cricut Maker machine and cut your projects!

Space Design is an application that works with intelligent cutting machines of the Cricut Maker and Cricut Explore family. Browse thousands of images, ready-made projects, and fonts in the Cricut Library. Or design your project from the ground up.

Properties:

• Design and cut DIY projects with the cutting machines Cricut Explore and Cricut Maker

• Choose from more than 50,000 images, fonts and projects in the Cricut image library or use your images and fonts for FREE.

• Upload your pictures and create them

• Design and cut without fonts and images downloaded to your device.

• Cut ready-made Make It Now projects quickly and easily.

• Design home and party design, cards and invitations, scrapbooking, fashion, jewelry, children's craft and more

• Cut a variety of materials, including paper, vinyl, ironing materials, cardboard, poster board, textiles, and even thicker materials such as leather.

• Use your device's built-in camera to position and visualize your projects against a realistic background.

• Log in with your Cricut ID to access your images and projects and easily pay for purchases at Cricut.com or Design Space.

• Bluetooth® wireless feature (Bluetooth adapter may be required, sold separately)

How to delete uploaded images in Cricut Design Space

1- Load up Cricut design space and Create a new project.

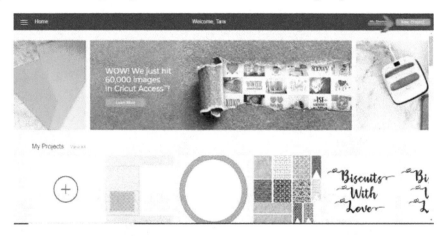

2- Click on the images icon.

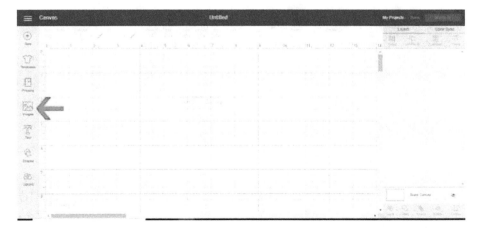

3- Click on the search icon and type in the name of the uploaded file you need to delete.

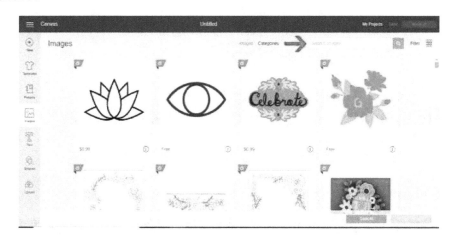

4- Once your file has appeared. Click on the information icon.

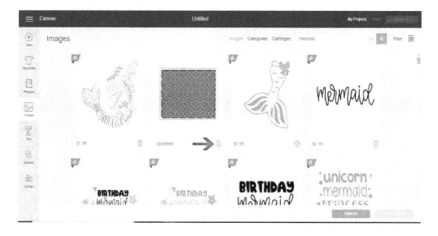

5- The information of the uploaded file will be listed and the option to delete. Click on delete.

6- A new pop up will appear. It will ask you to confirm the delete. Click yes.

7- The uploaded image is now removed.

How to use filters to find uploaded files in Cricut Design Space

1- Open the Cricut Design Space and click New Project.

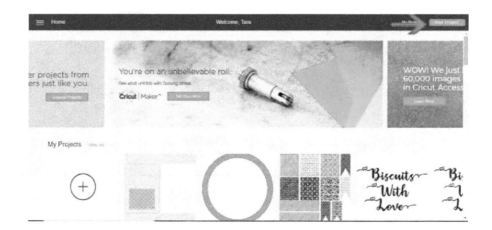

2- Click the download tool.

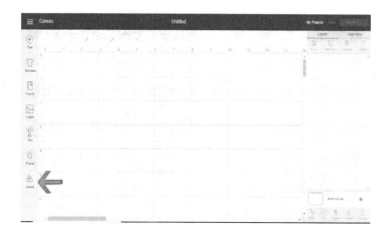

3- You will see the last downloads on your download screen. If you want to find all the downloads, click the Show All icon.

How to use Silhouette files in Cricut Design Space

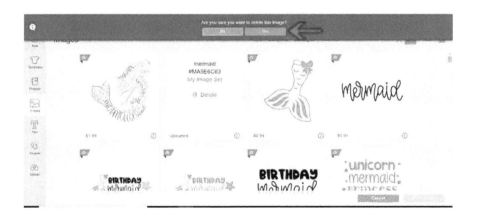

4- All images you download are displayed on the screen. You can then scroll to find the downloaded file you need.

5- You can also switch to the images icon and then click the filter option.

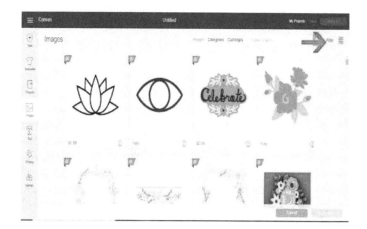

6- Select the download box from the drop-down list.

7- All downloaded files are now displayed. Select the downloaded design you need, and it will appear in your workspace.

How to use Silhouette files in Cricut Design Space

1- Open silhouette. Click on the library.

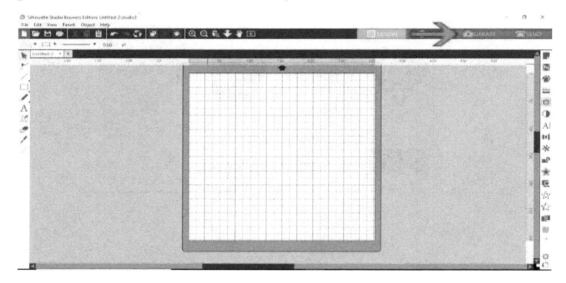

2- Locate the Silhouette file you want to use in the Cricut design area. Double click on it.

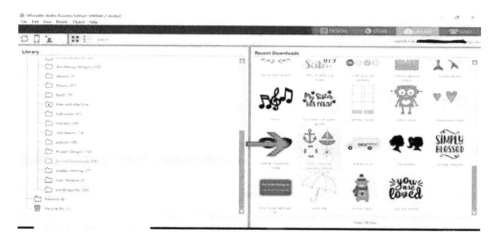

3- The file is displayed in the workspace. Click the line style tool.

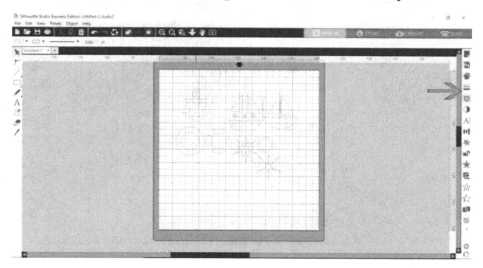

4- Select the black line.

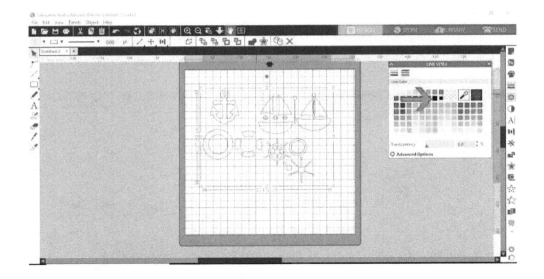

5- Click on the fill tool. Fill with black.

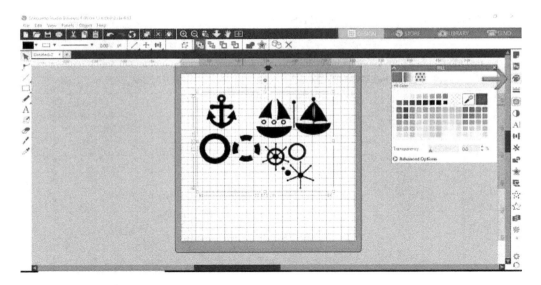

6- Select the layout icon. Click the grid options.

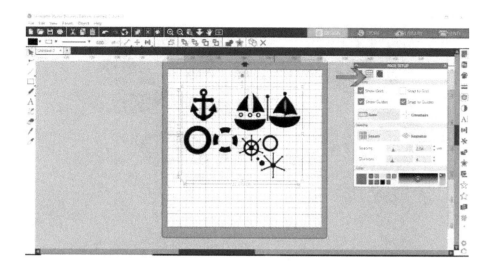

7- Remove the lines from the grid.

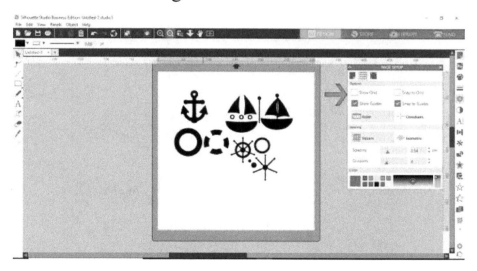

8- Take a screenshot of the design. Save the file in JPEG format.

9- Open the SPACE of de Cricut. Click on the new project.

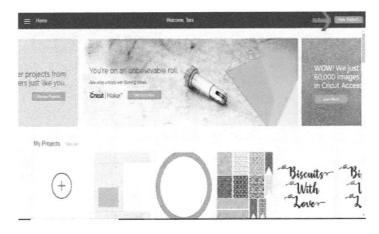

10- Select the download icon.

11- Click Download Image.

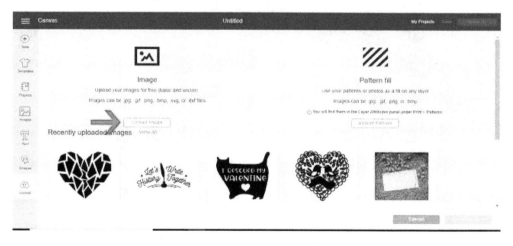

12- Click Browse. Select your screenshot.

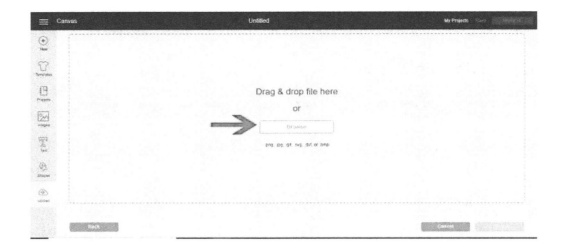

13- The screenshot will be displayed in your download window. Choose the easy option and continue.

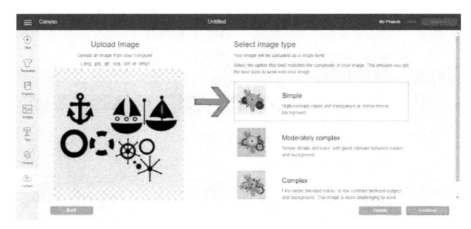

14- Use the Magic Wand tool to clear the background of the pattern. Then click Next.

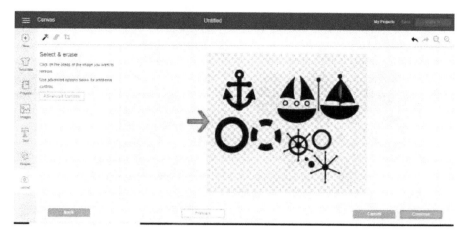

15 - You now have two options. To print and cut or simply import cut files. Select the cut the files and save.

16- The Silhouette file is now in a workspace of the Cricut Design section. Click on it.

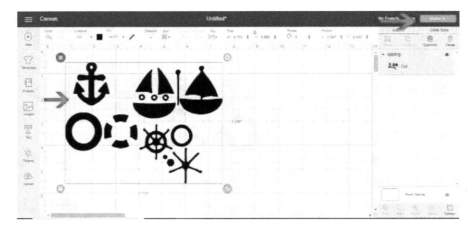

17- You can now cut out the Silhouette file in your Cricut machine.

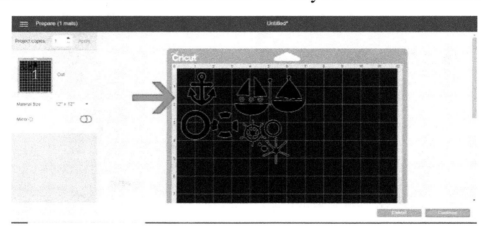

How to center your designs to cut in Cricut Design Space

1- Sign in to the Cricut Design section. Click on the new project.

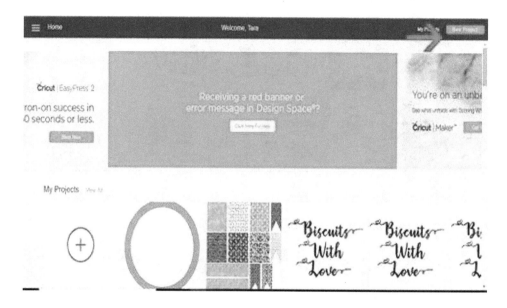

2- Click Download.

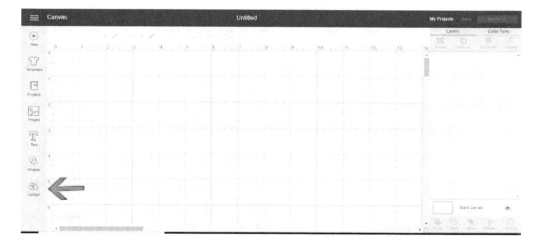

3- Click Upload Picture.

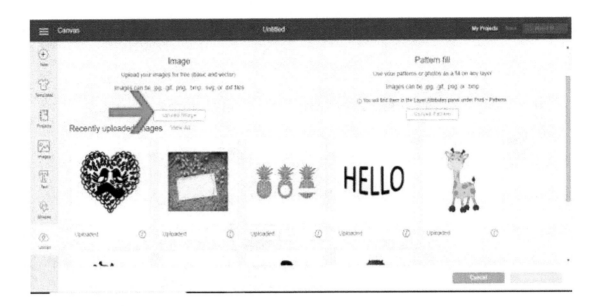

4- Click Browse.

5- Save your picture

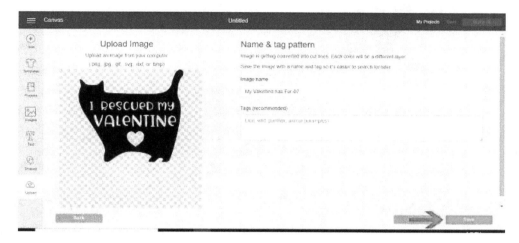

6- Select the saved image and insert an image.

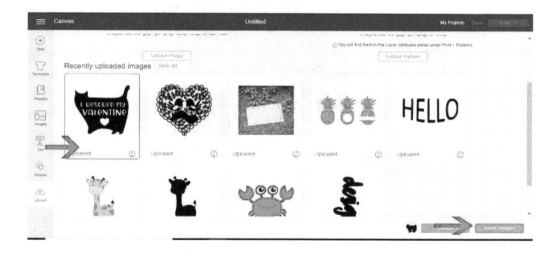

7- Select the picture. Click on it.

8- As you can see, the picture is automatically moved to the upper left corner.

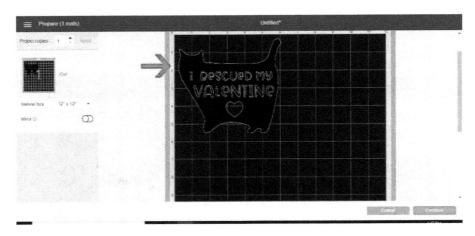

9- To prevent this, you can fool the software by placing the image in the center of your design area and the mat. This is useful if you want to create openings in the middle of a page.

Click on the shape tool.

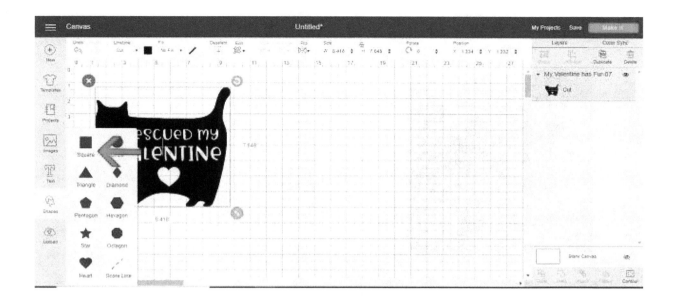

10- Create a shape of 11.5 x 11.5 inches.

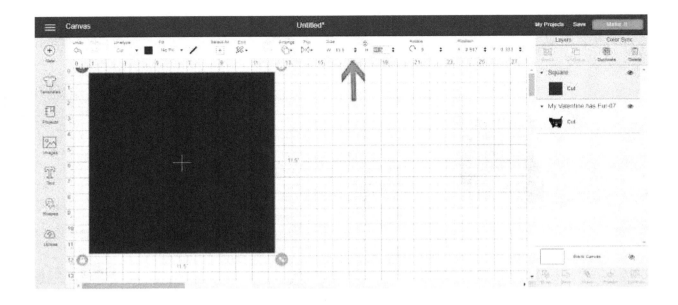

11- Select the square and change the setting to cut it in the drawing.

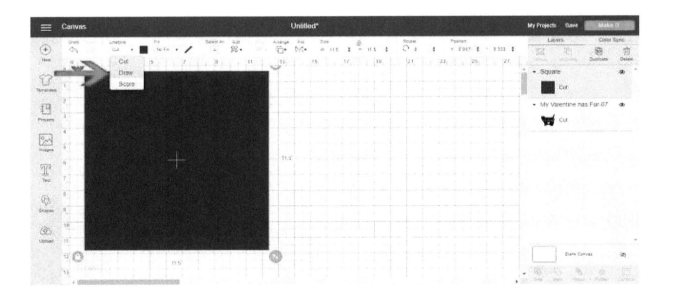

12- The square now appears as an outline.

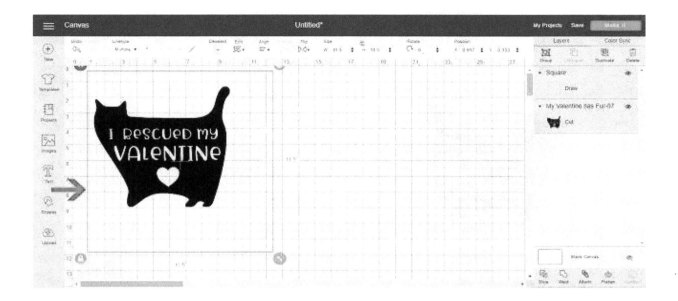

13- Click Align and Center with the selected pattern and square.

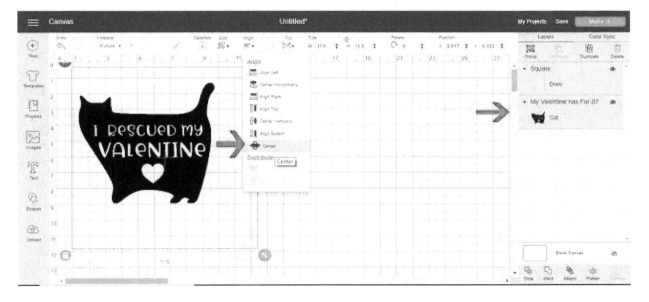

14- Click the arrow of the size of your square and resize it without moving the top left corner to reduce the size of the square.

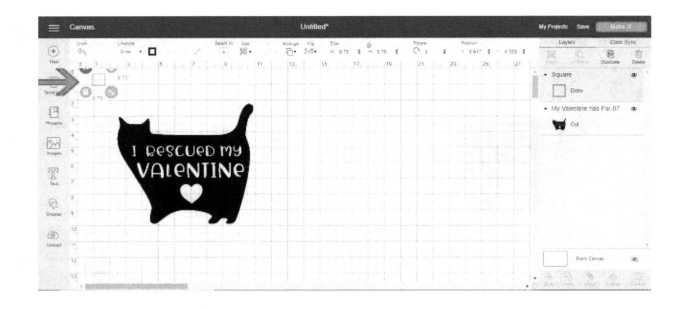

15- Select the square and pattern, then click Attach. Click on it.

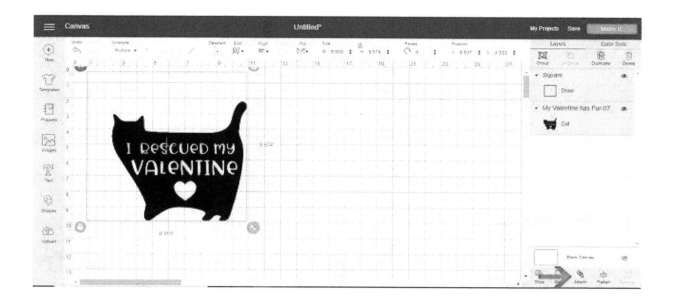

16- As you can see now, the design is centered.

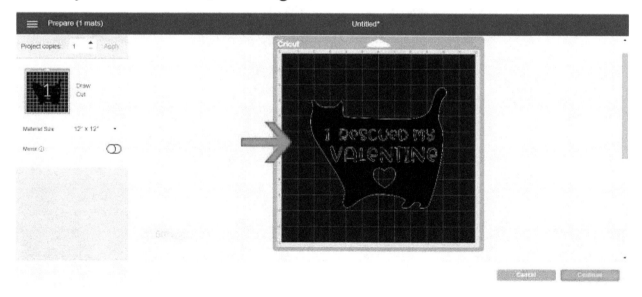

How to write with sketch pens in Cricut Design Space

1- Sign in to the Cricut Design section. Create a new project.

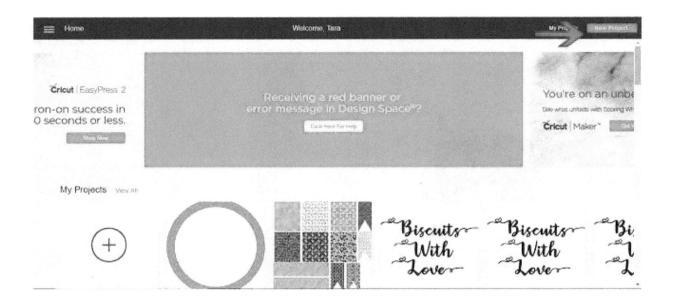

2- Click Download.

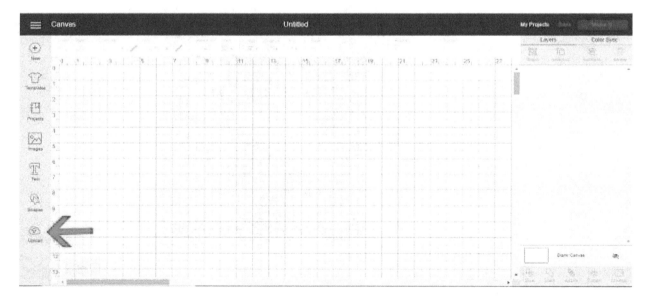

3- Select upload a picture.

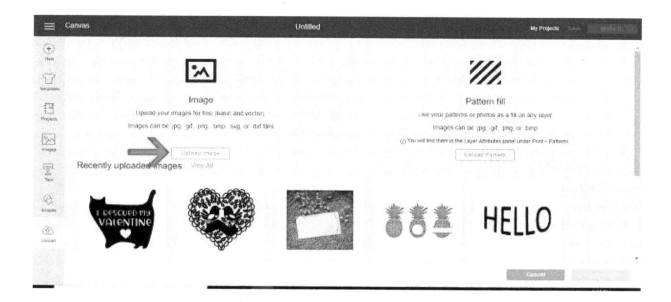

4- Click Browse.

5- open your file. Then save To get a good effect, use a file with thin lines and no large spaces.

6- Click on the pattern and paste it.

7- Select the pattern.

8- Change the drawing to a drawing.

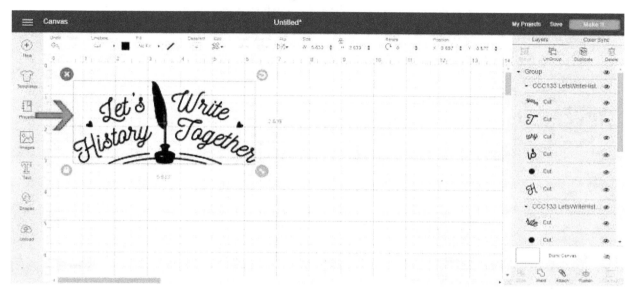

9- You will now see the drawing as an outline drawn.

Click on it.

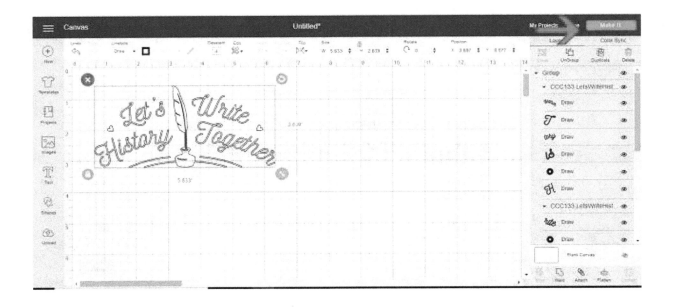

10- Your drawing will now be displayed on the cutting screen. Click on Continue.

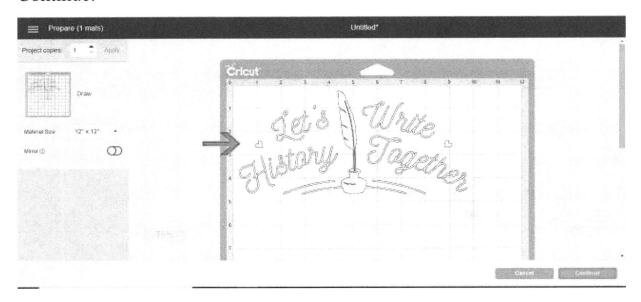

11- If you change your drawing to draw, the software automatically selects the pen tool. Insert the pen or marker into the recommended clip. Insert paper and click on the start icon.

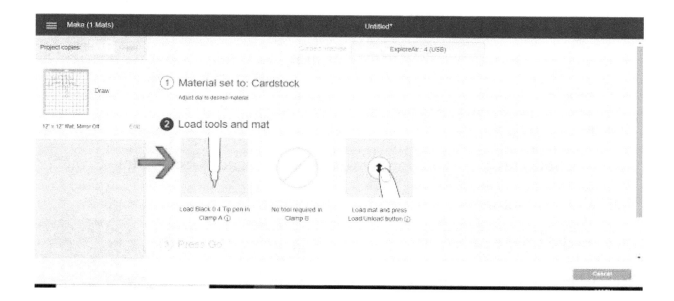

12- The pen now draws your pattern.

HOW TO UPLOAD PNG FILE IN CRICUT® DESIGN SPACE

After you've converted your PDF document to PNG file format, there are some ways to clean up the file before printing and then crop it with Cricut® Design Space.

Open Cricut® Design Space in your browser and click Create New Project.

Click Upload Picture.

Click on the image to upload

Click Browse

The Open dialog box opens. Select the PNG file you want to upload and click

An example of a picture can be found in Cricut® Design Space. Since we want to edit this file, we select Complex Image and click Next

The PNG file is loaded into Cricut® Design Space. Select and Delete

Select the selection and deletion tool and click anywhere on the white background, but not in any of the captions. I would suggest simply clicking on the white background in the upper right corner of the picture. The background is then magically erased. You can see that the background has been deleted because you now see the blue and white check marks (which show a transparent background) where the white background should be used.

While the Select and Delete tool is still selected, you want to click on each of the five gift tags in the small circles. Make sure you do not click on the tag itself. When you do this, click the undo arrow to the left of the zoom buttons.

Now click on the button Delete. You then want to magnify the eraser by sliding the slider to the right.

After selecting the slider, you can delete the text at the top and bottom of the page by clicking and dragging it with the mouse. When you have deleted all the text, click Next.

After loading the image, select Save as Print and then Cut Image. This is also a good time to add appropriate tags for your image so you can easily find them the next time you use this file. Then click on the green Save button.

After you have converted your PDF to PNG, uploaded the PNG in Cricut®, made changes (removed text and background) and saved the new PNG, you can cut Cricut!

HOW TO CONVERT A PDF IN PNG FORMAT

After downloading the PDF document to your computer, open your browser and go to png2pdf.com.

Click on the upload files

The "Open File" dialog box starts. Locate the PDF file to convert (probably in the Downloads folder), click the PDF file and click

The file is uploaded. You should see a progress bar. Once the file has been uploaded and converted, a Download button appears below the small image of the uploaded file. Click on the download

The file is downloaded as a ZIP file and appears in the status bar at the bottom of the screen. Just click on the filename to open the ZIP file.

The Open File dialog opens, and the downloaded file should be displayed. Since the file is still in ZIP format, you must first unzip or unzip it. Just click Extract All Files.

You will be asked where you want to save the extracted (extracted) file. You can accept the default location or click the Browse button to select the location where you want to save the file. Click Unpack

The Open File dialog opens, and your newly converted PDF file should be displayed in PNG file. You can open the file with a double-click if you only want to see what the file looks like. Close the window now by clicking on the red X.

After you have converted your PDF file to PNG format, you must upload the PNG file to Cricut® Design Space so that you can use the Print and Cut functions.

HOW TO USE OF PRINT THEN CUT WITH UPLOADED PICTURES-.JPG

1. Click New Project. You can do this by selecting the green box on the top right or the + in My Projects.

Start a new design project.

2. Upload your JPG by clicking the Upload button on the left. This will bring you to the next screen where you can choose to upload an image.

Upload the new file to the Cricut Design section

3. Select Browse and locate your JPG file on your computer. Click Open.

4. You will then choose your image type based on your design. (I choose 95% of the time Complex) Then click Next on the bottom right.

Upload JPG image - Select complex - Click Next

The next screen is "Select" and "Delete" and looks like .jpg in front and the middle.

Step 2. Select excess areas - Delete

5. Here we tell your Cricut where to cut. Use the mouse to select the areas around the image you want to "delete." Click on Continue.

Step 2a. Select the areas that you want to delete in your JPG

6. This will show you what the cut file will look like. If you want to make adjustments, choose Back. If this is correct, select Save as Print and then Cut Image. Add the correct tags (this will help with a new search!) And then click Save in the lower right corner.

3. Review - save as cut and print

7. Finally, you can select the print and then cut the image and paste it into the bottom of your project screen using the Insert Images button in the bottom right corner.

4. Upload picture

8. I then adjusted my picture. (Not larger than 9.25 "x 6.75") Note that the line type is cut out and the fill is printed. That's exactly what we want. Click Make It in the upper-right corner of your screen.

5. Resize - Create

9. Now you can print and cut! On the matte screen, you can see how to put your printed design on your mat. Do not be disturbed by the black border.

Your Cricut reads these rules and knows where to cut! Click Next in the lower right corner.

6. Matte screen - Click Next

10. Connect your device above. (Any machine, Explore or higher works!) Select Send to Printer and select the printer and print.

7. Connect a device - send to the printer

11. A printer dialog appears where you can find your printer at home and select the number of copies. Normally, I stop the bleeding. This will ensure that you do not get a white border around your design. Click Print

8. Print

Your picture will be printed on your home printer. I like to print on cardboard.

Print Printer prints and trims the image

Now we choose our material. I use Cardstock for this project.

9. Select material

We are ready to load our mat into our machine! Apply your printed image to your Cricut mat. (I like to use the Blue LightGrip Mat for Cardstock) And load it into your machine as if you were cutting something else.

10. Place the mat on and cut it off

Insert the mat in Cricut

Press Go (the flashing Cricut "C")!

Your device reads the black lines on all four sides. When using the maker, the carriage will move to the right to "spot" the tool (make sure the knife with the fine tip is inside) and then start cutting your constructions! When done, remove it from the machine.

Carefully remove the excess cardboard and voila!

Remove excess design

Project completed

HOW TO USE PRINT THEN CUT FUNCTION IN THE CRICUT DESIGN SPACE-.PNG:

PNG files are slightly faster to use than JPG files because PNG files usually have a transparent background. If your PNG file does not have a transparent background, follow the instructions for the JPG files.

1. Click New Project. You can do this by selecting the green box on the top right or the + in My Projects.

Start a new design project

2. Upload your PNG by clicking the Upload button on the left. This will bring you to the next screen where you can choose to upload an image.

Upload the new file to the Cricut Design section

3. Select Browse and locate your PNG file on your computer. Click Open.

To use the Cricut Print and Cut feature.

4. You can see below that we have a transparent background because you can see the checkerboard pattern. Choose the image type based on your design. (I choose 95% of the time Complex) Then click Next on the bottom right.

Upload your PNG file

5. The next screen is "Select" and "Delete" and looks like this with your .png front and center. Since our background is already transparent, we have nothing to do here. Click on Continue.

No background to delete

6. This will show you what the cut file will look like. If you want to make adjustments, choose Back. If this is correct, select Save as Print and then Cut Image. Add the correct tags (this will help with a new search!) And then click Save in the lower right corner.

Add tags select Next.

7. Finally, you can select the print and then cut the image and paste it into the bottom of your project screen using the Insert Images button in the bottom right corner.

Select a file and click on "Insert images."

8. I then adjusted my picture. (Not larger than 9.25 "x 6.75") Note that the line type is cut out and the fill is PRINT. That's exactly what we want. Click Make It in the upper-right corner of your screen.

Change image size

9. Now you can print and cut! On the matte screen, you can see how to put your printed design on your mat. Do not be disturbed by the black border. Your Cricut reads these rules and knows where to cut! Click Next in the lower right corner.

10. Connect your device above. (Any machine, Explore or higher works!) Select Send to Printer and select the printer and print.

11. A printer dialog appears where you can find your printer at home and select the number of copies. Normally, I stop the bleeding. This will ensure that you do not get a white border around your design. Click Print

Your picture will be printed on your home printer.

We are ready to load our mat into our machine! Apply your printed image to your Cricut mat. (I like to use the Blue LightGrip Mat for Cardstock) and load it into your machine as if you were cutting something else.

Press Go (the flashing Cricut "C")!

Your device reads the black lines on all four sides. When using the maker, the carriage will move to the right to "spot" the tool (make sure the knife with the fine tip is inside) and then start cutting your constructions! When done, remove it from the machine.

Carefully remove the excess cardboard and voila! Project completed

HOW TO USE PRINT THEN CUT FUNCTION WITH CRICUT DESIGN SPACE IMAGES:

1. Click New Project. You can do this by selecting the green box on the top right or the + in My Projects.

Start a new design project

2. Click the Images icon in the left toolbar to begin.

3. Browse Cricut Design Space for your perfect picture! You can search for pictures, categories or cassettes. In addition to using the search bar, there is also a printable filter. (Printouts are ready to use as a printable image that you do not need to convert.

Select your picture and click on "Insert pictures."

4. Here you can see the drawing on our canvas as a cut file, which is indicated by all cut-out layers in the layer bar on the right.

5. If you switch to printing and then want to cut, just select all the layers. Select them individually in the Layers panel, or drag a large box around the entire image to select everything. We then click on the Layers tool at the bottom of the Layers panel.

6. Now you can see that we have converted it to expression and then converted it as a cropped image since all the cut planes in the Layer window are in a section | have been changed to print level. Change the size if necessary. The maximum size for printing and subsequent cutting is 6.75 "x 9.25". Click Make It in the upper right corner.

7. The following is the matte screen. This shows us how we put the imprint on our mat. Do not be disturbed by the black border. The Cricut reads these black lines to determine where to cut. Click on Continue.

8. Next, plug in your device at the top of the screen. Every machine that is an Explore or higher works with Print and Cut. Then click Send to Printer.

9. A pop-up printer screen appears, allowing you to connect your home network printer and select the number of copies you need: Click Print, and the design prints on your home printer.

10. Then select your material.

11. Now it's time to load your mat. Place the printed motif on your mat and load it into your machine.

12. You can now cut "C" on your machine by pressing the flashing Cricut.

The sensor on our machine reads the black lines on all four sides. When using the maker, the carriage will move to the right to "spot" the tool (make sure the knife with the fine tip is inside) and then start cutting your constructions! When done, remove it from the machine.

Carefully remove the excess material and voila! Project completed

HOW TO USE OF PRINT THEN CUT FUNCTION WITH TEXT:

1. Click New Project. You can do this by selecting the green box on the top right or the + in My Projects.

Start a new design project

2. To get started, click the text icon in the left toolbar.

3. Write your text in the text box. Then use the Text toolbar to customize the font, size, letter spacing, ink, and more.

4. There are now two ways to convert text to an image and then print it. If you are working with a single layer, change the FILL from "Do not fill" to "Print."

If you work with more than one layer, you can do the same as above for each layer, or you can select all layers and use the flattening tool at the bottom of the Layer window.

This will cut them into layers and then cut them. Click Make It in the upper right corner.

5. The following is the matte screen. This shows us how we put the imprint on our mat. Do not be disturbed by the black border. The Cricut reads these black lines to determine where to cut. Click on Continue.

6. Then connect your device to the top of the screen. Every machine that is an Explore or higher works with Print and Cut. Then click Send to Printer.

HOW TO CURVE TEXT ON THE CRICUT DESIGN SPACE

You open a text box on your canvas screen. To do this, select the text tool in the left toolbar. A box will open, and you can enter your text.

The Text Editing toolbar lets you choose your font, adjust distance, size, etc. (see below for my tips).

Then select your text and click on the curve text tool.

The best way to create crooked text on Cricut

A box is opened with a box with a slider and a numeric type. You can adjust the curve by moving the slider to the left or right or by entering the diameter directly in the type field.

Create curved text in Cricut Design Space

To create a curve, move the opposite direction by moving the slider to the left or by entering a negative value in the text box.

FREQUENTLY ASKED QUESTIONS FOR PRINT THEN CUT FUNCTION WITH CRICUT DESIGN SPACE:

Is the Cricut printed for printing and then a project cut

No. You need a printer at home to print. They will cut Cricut. The Cricut machine can draw. You can read more about this in my article on using the Cricut Pens.

What materials can you use with Print and then cut?

In short, all the material you can input through your printer. Some examples are cardboard, paper, sticker paper, self-adhesive vinyl, printable vinyl on iron and parchment.

Can I use colored materials?

Colored materials, such. Colored cards are only recommended for the Cricut Maker because it has an improved sensor.

Which machines have the print and cut function?

Printing and cutting are available on all Explore family machines (Explore, Explore Air, Explore Air 2) and the Cricut Maker machine.

Can I use the Print & Cut feature on designs printed from a location other than my home computer?

No. You must print from Design Space

TIPS FOR USING THE CURVE TEXT TOOL FOR CRICUT

This tool is currently only available on the desktop. It is not available for cell phones or tablets.

The curved text is also not displayed on the phone or tablet unless the text is welded or flattened so that it is a picture and not a text box.

Bent text can be fully edited (unless it is welded, flattened or ungrouped, and regrouped). It is recommended that you first curl your text and then adjust, rotate, edit, or change the font spacing. Etc.

This tool only works for individual lines of text. If you want to bend multiple lines, you must type them one at a time or use the Split Group to Lines tool to separate the lines into their text boxes.

HOW TO USE SVG'S IN THE CRICUT DESIGN SPACE:

1. Download your SVG file to a place that you can remember and access.

2. Open Cricut Design Space and log in. If you do not have a Cricut ID, you can create one in this step.

3. Click on "New Project" in the upper right corner of the screen (green button) or on the lower left corner.

Start a new project in Cricut Design Space.

4. A blank canvas opens, and we click the Upload Images button on the left side of the toolbar.

Upload SVGs to the Cricut Design Space

5. In the next screen, we can choose to upload a picture or a pattern. We choose the left side and upload an image. (Image is defined as multiple file types, including .svg files!)

Upload your SVG files to Cricut Design Space

6. Select Browse to locate the folder where you saved your SVG in step 1.

How do I use an SVG in Cricut Design Space?

6. After selecting your saved SVG file, a screen will appear at the bottom. You may want to edit the title and add the desired tags. (noted with 1.) This helps to later create your library when sorting your projects and files. Then choose "Save" (noted with 2.)

Upload tags to your new SVG file and add them

7. You will now see that your new SVG design is in first place in the "Recently uploaded images" section (marked with 1). Select this picture and then click on "Insert Pictures" in the lower right corner.

8. This will place your SVG file on your blank canvas in Design Space.

Upload SVG to Cricut

Then you can follow the steps in this Gratitude Journal to load the mat and cut your vinyl, or in this Boy's Valentine shirt, if you're using heat transfer!

HOW TO MAKE A MONOGRAM IN THE CRICUT DESIGN SPACE

Download your favorite monogram font

Open Cricut Design Space on a blank canvas.

Enter your first name with the text tool.

Select your font (Monogram) with the first text in the Fonts drop-down list in the Text Layer area. I love this first initial at 1.25 inches.

Cricut Design Space screenshot that shows where the font and height of the original character should be changed

If this start is selected, click Duplicate in the Layers panel and change the text to the middle initial letter.

Repeat step 5 for the LAST start and change the size to 1.75 inches.

Cricut design space Screenshot of the first initials of Center Monogram

To align, I will first select all three initials and align the vertical centers of the letters. From there I can adjust if necessary with the mouse or the arrow keys.

Cricut Design Space screenshot of using the Align tool

We want our machine to cut this design as a solid piece and not cut each piece separately, so we all weld them together to get a solid design. Select all three initials and select the WELD tool at the bottom of the Layers panel.

Cricut Design Space screenshot of using the welding tool

Do it! Cut your finished design! If you think you will use this again, do not forget that you can SAVE it in your projects in Cricut Design Space.

NOTE: Do not forget to MIRROR your design if you use iron-on transfer paper!

TOP TIPS AND TRICKS: THE BASIC PRINCIPLES OF THE CRICUT DESIGN ROOM

Option "New"

Use this option at any time to start a new project and get a blank canvas. After clicking on it, you will be asked if you want to save your current project or replace it with a blank canvas.

Templates Tool

Here you can set a specific type of template to illustrate what your design looks like for a particular element. This can be useful for plotting and sizing. The template will not be cut out. I usually only use a blank canvas, but that's just my preference.

For some templates, you can tailor the dimension to your work in the drop-down menu. In the following example, the size of the apron can be changed from Adult to Kid

Projects

Use this option to see all available Ready to Make projects. These are projects that have already been completed for you, and you can easily create them! Some projects can be customized as you open them.

You can search for projects that are included in Cricut Access by using the drop-down menu. There are also other categories like "Free for Cricut Explore" or "Free for Cricut Maker." You can try these free projects if you only learn how to operate your machine.

Insert image tool

When you click the Pictures tool, the Cricut Library opens with pictures. Here you can choose from thousands of images that you can insert into your project. To narrow your selection in the upper right corner, there is a search option that lets you search for a specific image. The images with the green "a" in the left corner are included in your Cricut Access (click HERE to learn more about Cricut Access.)

Another useful option is to search in specific categories or cassettes. If you have used an older Cricut cartridge, you can look it up. You can also search for categories like "flower."

text tool

If you select this option, a text box is displayed, and you can enter the desired text. The text you enter is then displayed on your canvas.

If you want to edit your text, use the options in the top toolbar when your text is selected.

You can change your font in the first drop-down list. You can choose between All fonts, System fonts (i.e., fonts on your computer), or Cricut fonts for browsing. You can also use the search bar to search for a specific font.

A nice feature is the use of the filter option on the far right of the text menu. This is how you can filter your search. You can only select one or more filters, for example, My fonts and writing. This then only shows results that meet both criteria. Write is a great filter to filter on when looking for fonts that can be used with your Cricut pens. In the following example, I have selected "My Fonts" and "Write" as the filter. Therefore, only these two criteria are met. Just click the options again to deselect them in your filters.

Multilevel fonts have a shadow. When you enter your text, the shadow level is hidden by default. You can simply click the eye icon to see the shadow. I've selected a multilayer font below, but the shadow layer fades until I click on the eye icon and fade it back in.

You will also notice some other text options, such as: As a font, font size, letter and line area, and orientation. These are options that you are probably used to, but you can click around for a few minutes to familiarize yourself with these options.

Letter Space is an excellent tool for using italic letters that are closer together and should touch. Just decrease the letter spacing by selecting the down arrow. You can see that I have reduced the letter for the word below. The font I selected below is a "Write" font. This means that I can use pens to write when creating my project. Fonts without writing style form the structure of the text (the text is not filled in when creating a project).

Another important tool is the button with insulating letters. You can use this to edit each letter individually in your text. I use this to rotate my letters when the text is to be bent. Or if I want a particular letter to be larger than the rest. You can also select your text on the canvas and right-click on it to select Ungroup, which does the same thing. Once you have edited the text, select it again, right-click, and click a group so that all the text can be moved and edited again.

Shapes tool

You can use this option to include basic shapes such as a circle, square, heart, etc. in your design. I'll go into more detail on how to edit these shapes later.

Upload Tool

Here you can upload your pictures and designs. If you click on it, the following screen appears.

Layer menu

When you open the Layers menu on the right side of your screen, several options are displayed at the bottom: Segment, Weld, Confirm, Smooth, and Outline. This is important when creating your designs.

Segment - Split two overlapping layers into parts

Welding - Merge multiple layers into one shape

Confirm: Hold pictures in the cut position, or add text to the picture layer

Collapse - Merge layers in a printable image

Contour - Hide / Show your lines on one level

The Layers menu displays all the different texts and images you have on your canvas. Each is a separate layer. When you click one of the layers, a menu bar named Layer Attributes appears. Here you can change the properties of the selected layer.

There are four different options: Cut, Write, Sheet and Print. If you look at the right side of your layer, which I have selected in the picture, you will see the scissors with the circle symbol next to it. This means that your circle is currently set to cut. If you choose another option, such as writing, this small icon changes to the letter symbol, a circle with a small tip. If you select the Print option, the circle is printed instead of being cut or written.

Color Synchronization Tool

Another option is the color synchronization tool. It has a brief description right in the menu, what you do when you select it. You can drag and drop different layers to give them the same color. This is useful when cutting out projects with multiple colors, as this guarantees that you will cut all the pieces of the same color at the same time. This saves you the time to switch back and forth between the material you are cutting, as you are cutting the same color at the same time!

When you insert a shape or design, you can click on the small lock below in the lower left corner to unlock the shape. This allows you to customize the shape. If you want a precise size, you can also select the shape and change the numbers in the menu above. There are also options to turn your shape or bring it to an exact position.

Attach

If you want Cricut to remove something on your canvas, remove the Append option. Many people are frustrated when they press the Go button to cut, and their design is moved by the program to cut to save material. To avoid this problem, choose Attach.

Slice

If you have two layers, you can select both and choose the Insert button, which divides the layers into sections as shown in the picture below. (Make sure the desired layers are selected, as shown in blue in the Layers menu.)

How to solve Cricut design space problems

1. Slow internet connection

The main cause of problems with Design Space is a slow Internet connection. The program requires good and consistent upload and download speeds. An inconsistent connection with dips and spikes can also cause problems with the software. You'll probably get a more consistent connection if your device is closer to your modem.

Websites like YouTube require good download speeds, and you can get away with slower upload speed. However, Cricut Design Space requires both download and upload speeds as you constantly send and receive information while working on your design.

Perform a speed test

Perform an internet speed test

Cricut sets the following requirements for Design Space to function properly:

Broadband Connection

Download at least 2 - 3 MBit / s

At least 1 - 2 Mbps upload

2. Your computer

If this is not your Internet speed, the problem may be with the computer, tablet, or mobile device you're using. Minimum requirements for Design Space are recommended for the proper operation of Design Space. These are the basic principles:

Windows computer

Your Windows computer must:

runs under Windows 8 or higher

have Intel Core Series or AMD processor - mine has AMD and works great

Have 4GB of RAM

at least 50 MB free hard disk space - the more, the better

have a free USB port or a Bluetooth connection

Apple Computer

Your Mac computer needs the following for Design Space to work:

Mac OS X 10.12 or later

a CPU of 1.83 GHz

Have 4GB of RAM

Have 50 MB of free space

an available USB port or Bluetooth capabilities

Background programs

Another problem may be that too many background programs are running while you try to use Design Space.

Watch Netflix at the same time, chat on Facebook, keep your mom, download the last season of Fixer Upper, upload your current vlog to YouTube, and try designing a design in Design Space? Besides earning a medal, since you can accomplish so much at the same time, you must close some programs to make DS run smoothly.

But seriously, it can be the problem, even if you do not do everything. Sometimes closing things you do not use becomes faster.

Other things that can help

Here are a few other things that you want to test or complete:

Empty your cache and your story

Check what your antivirus software does and update it if necessary

Update drivers (for Windows)

defrag your hard drive

Run a malware review

3. your browser

Another possible cause of your Design Space issues may be your browser.

Cricut states that you must use the latest version of a particular browser. Whether you're using Chrome, Mozilla, Firefox, or Edge, make sure it's up to date. If a browser does not work, check if it works in another browser. Sometimes the problem can be solved for unknown reasons.

4. Call Cricut

If all else fails, you may need to call Cricut Customer Support to discuss your specific problem.

CHAPTER 6: SUBSCRIPTION ON CRICUT

What is Cricut Access?

Cricut Access is an optional monthly (or annual) subscription that allows you to access a large number of images and fonts in Cricut Design Space that you would otherwise have to pay for

You may remember your free trial at first use. If you're like me, it was over before you could really figure out what it was and if you needed it.

Let's take a look at the most frequently asked questions about Cricut Access.

Do I have access to CRICUT to use my CRICUT?

Many users, especially newer ones, do not know if they can use their Cricut Design Space without a subscription. The answer is ABSOLUTELY! As mentioned earlier, there are three other ways to get images for Design Space.

DO I NEED CRICUT ACCESS?

Honestly, I do not know. It is such an individual thing, and every human being must decide according to its use. If you have different projects, use your Cricut computer regularly and often need to buy pictures. Subscribing can be a good choice for you. On the other hand, if you are an occasional user, you tend to run the same types of projects with the same designs, or if you use many SVGs, this may not be a real benefit to you. Price.

WHAT IS IN ACCESS TO CRICUT? HOW MUCH DOES IT COST?

There are currently three levels of Cricut Access subscriptions: Cricut Access font, Cricut Access Standard and Cricut Access Premium.

Cricut Access Fonts - The font subscription is the cheapest option. It costs $ 59.88 a year ($ 4.99 a month) or $ 6.99 a month. You have access to more than 400 fonts.

I think it's a great option, as the fonts not only buy full sets of pictures but are also the most expensive ones (usually $ 4.99 or $ 6.99 apiece). Of course, you can also use any system fonts on your computer or device for free, but there are really cute Cricut fonts! It's also much easier than downloading and installing system fonts.

Cricut Access Standard - The standard subscription includes all subscription fonts, but also provides access to more than 30,000 images (some of which are for the Access subscription only) and more than 1,000 projects.

The standard subscription also includes two discounts. First, 10% off the purchase of images and licensed fonts. (License models such as Mickey Mouse are not part of an Access subscription.) The other discount is a 10%

discount on all product purchases on the Cricut website and can be combined with other available discounts.

Standard access costs $ 95.88 per annum or $ 7.99 per month. With monthly payment, the price is $ 9.99. I believe that for an additional cost of $ 3 per month, any additional benefits will be used to upgrade the default character set subscription.

Cricut Access Premium - Premium Subscription is the only subscription for which no monthly payment option is available. It's $ 119.88, or $ 9.99 a month. It contains all the fonts, images and discounts of Cricut Access Standard.

The Premium Access subscription also offers a 50% discount on all images and everyday fonts that are not included in Access. (It is important to know that the discount does not apply in the app, but can only be combined on a desktop computer or the Cricut website and also not with other discounts.) Other benefits include exclusive offers and sales, which are exclusive to Premium Access members, as well as free shipping on orders over $ 50.

REASONS YOU NEED CRICUT ACCESS

NO DESIGN EXPERIENCE REQUIRED WITH CRICUT ACCESS PROJECTS

You will enjoy working on Make It Now projects because you just press a few buttons. You will see how you do this to create the beautiful gift boxes you see in the picture above. You can use any paper, and the Cricut does all the work for you!

PERSONALIZE GRAPHICS IN ACCESS TO CRICUT

Again, this may require little or no design experience, but you can customize the Make It Now projects or other Cricut Access library graphics.

GREAT GRAPHIC LIBRARY

Cricut contains more than 30,000 images in Cricut Access! They have also greatly facilitated the search for images. If you want a specific graphic, Cricut Access probably has one in your subscription. It contains simple images, 3D projects, multi-layered images and more! You will have instant access to all these images as soon as you have registered.

Large font library

In addition to graphics and projects, Cricut Access contains over 370 fonts! I love some fonts, so it's a big advantage for me. If you only use fonts, Cricut has a subscription to plain fonts!

DISCOUNT ON ARTWORK AND FONTS

Cricut offers incredible fonts and graphics that are accessible, but if you like something that you love in the store, you'll get a 50% off many items in

the store 10% off a standard subscription with a premium subscription. Note: The 50% discount does not include any items from certain licensed companies. Be sure to read what's included.

DISCOUNT ON PHYSICAL PRODUCTS FROM KRIKUT

If you do not receive the discount on digital products, you could have a 10% discount on physical products. If you create multiple Cricut projects per month, you save vinyl, mats, and other Cricut accessories with this subscription.

EXCLUSIVE SALES FOR MEMBERS ACCESS TO CRICUT

In addition to the daily savings, you will also be informed about promotions and exclusive sales. If you plan to create many projects with your Cricut every month, this can be very useful.

CHAPTER 7: FUNCTION KEYS OF CRICUT MACHINE

Your box should contain:

1. Cricut Expression ™ machine

2. User manual

3. Font Cartridge, Cartridge Binder, Overlay Keyboard,

and manually

4. Assembly of the blade

5. Cutting mat 30,48 cm x 30,48 cm (12 inch x 12 inch)

6. Quick guide

7. AC adapter

Cricut Expression ™ 24 "Personal Electronic Trimmer

The following will help you to become familiar with your Cricut Expression ™.

Machine.

Install the cutting blade assembly

Please note that the assembly of the cutting blade of the Cricut Expression ™ machine takes place

Located at the bottom of the box, separate from the machine. Before turning the

When the machine is on, you must insert the blade. Follow these instructions

simple instructions:

1. Open the doors of the Cricut printout

Machine and remove the cardboard inserts

on each side of the car.

2. Remove the green cutting blade

out of his pocket. Make sure the black arrow on the

The blade assembly points to # 4 on the

Adjust knob and make sure the cut

The blade was inserted into the assembly

the pointed end points downwards.

3. The blade unit fits into the black holder

on the left side of the car. Find the money

screw it in and turn it counterclockwise until it stops

Loosen enough for you to swing the screw

the right Be careful not to loosen the screw

a lot, or he will fall.

4. Open the left arm of the black cradle and

position the cutting knife inside as

with the black arrow pointed to you. Shut down

the cradle sweep the screw to the left,

and tighten by turning clockwise. Plug it in

Machine and press the on the button to place

the blade in the cutting position.

Position your Cricut Expression ™ machine

Make sure your Cricut Expression ™ machine is at least 12 inches (30.48 cm) from the edge of your device

to prevent it from tipping over and causing injury.

Depending on the cutting mat used

Let 12 "(30.48 cm) or 24" (60.96 cm) in

Back of the Cricut Expression Machine for

Carpet movement.

When positioning your Cricut Expression machine, select a location

• Inaccessible to children. The Cricut Expression machine is not a toy and contains

Components, including a sharp blade that could be dangerous to children.

• stable, even and hard surface, at a distance of 1.83 m from a grounded electrical contact

Exit and behind the Cricut has a minimum distance of 60.96 cm

ATTENTION! Your Cricut Expression ™ system should never be left out or stored.

unheated or non-air conditioned SPACEs or in environments where the machine or

The cartridges may come into contact with water.

What can your Cricut Expression ™ machine cut?

The Cricut Expression ™ cutting system can cut a variety of materials from Vellum

and cardboard on the whiteboard and vinyl. The Cricut Expression machine can even cut

Thin chipboard with multi-cut function. Learn more about the exciting

Possibilities with this function on page 18.

TIP: Repeatedly cutting heavy materials can shorten the life of the blade and carpet of your Cricut Expression ™ machine.

Expressing machine for paper movements.

Basic functions to install

-Connect your Cricut Expression ™ device to a grounded electrical outlet.

-Lift the Display board.

-Place the keyboard pad on top of the keyboard.

-Insert a Cricut ™ cartridge into the slot.

is located at the front of your Cricut Expression machine.

-Turn it on by pressing the ON button near the

CUT button.

-Loading Paper

TIP: The Cricut Expression Machine lets you cut materials up to 30,48 cm (12 "x 24").

60.96 cm). The machine can not cut materials less than 7,62 cm x 7,62 cm (3 "x 3").

Cardstock is recommended for best results. We recommend practicing less

expensive material while familiarizing yourself with the features described here

User Guide.

-Lay the paper on the cutting mat

-For the first test, a paper size of 12 "x 12" (30,48 cm x 30,48 cm) is recommended.

-Insert a Cricut ™ cartridge into the slot. It is located at the front of your Cricut

Expression machine.

-Turn it on by pressing the ON button near the

CUT button.

1. Remove the transparent protective cover from

cutting mat

2. Align one corner of the paper with the Align icon

Paper corner here »icon in the lower left corner

cutting mat

3. Press and smooth from the center of the Paper on the edges of the cutting
mat for Stick well your paper can be cut

Load the cutting mat into the machine

1. Once the paper has been laid on the carpet,

Put the carpet with the arrow in the machine

point to the machine.

2. Hold the cutting mat firmly between the roller

Bar and bridge and gently push the first one

Carpet edge in rolls. Then press the

Load the Paper button on the keyboard overlay. the

The Cricut Expression machine then loads the

Carpet and paper. If the carpet does not load, press

Unload the paper and try again.

Choose your characters

Select the character (s) you want to cut out of the keyboard overlay. Your selection will be

displayed on the screen.

Keys and basic keys to know

If you want to prevent the Cricut Expression ™ engine from cutting

Before the end just press the STOP button and the CUT button. This interrupts every ongoing process.

Press the CUT button to begin cutting the characters

the screen.

Use the Shift key to select the character in the top right corner

Corner of a key. The toggle button lights green when it is activated.

TIP: To select a character in the upper right corner of a key, press

Press the Shift key once (you do not have to hold down) and

Your selection

The Shift key allows repeated selection of characters in the list.

Upper right corners of the keys. The shift key is illuminated from behind

Green when active.

The space bar works just like the spacebar of a computer or

Typewriter space is inserted after the last entered character

every time you press the spacebar.

The backspace works just like the backspace key of a

Computer or typewriter. It deletes the characters from the last one

An entrance every time he is in a hurry.

The Clear Display key clears the contents of the Cricut expression

the display of the device when you press it.

The Reset All button clears the contents of the Cricut Expression.

Display the device and restore all defaults. No key

should light green after pressing Reset All.

The Last Repeat button inserts the last slice selections.

The display. Once the characters are displayed on the screen, you can do so

Press CUT again, or you can change the settings (properties, size of) Speed,

pressure, etc.) and then press CUT.

The Sound On / Off button turns the beep on or off. This key does not turn Disable the system warning tones.

The paper loading button pulls in the cutting mat and paper the machine

The Unload Paper button ejects the cutting mat and paper the machine Press only when the Cricut Expression machine is on finish cutting.

The Paper Size button is used when the paper size is used.

30,48 cm x 30,48 cm or 30,48 cm x 12 "x 24"

60.96 cm), depending on the size of the selected carpet. Insert the paper

Align on the cutting mat and align in the lower left corner of the carpet

(even if you're cropping in portrait mode). Once the paper has

Place the arrow on the carpet and place it in the rug first

Hold the machine and hold firmly between the roller and the deck.

Then tap Load paper. Move the blade to the top right

Paper edge with the navigation buttons on the blade and then

Press the Set Paper Size button. The size of your paper will be displayed on display. You can now enter information for your project.

Finally, use the Load button instead of the paper key

You have temporarily unloaded the carpet, and you want the blade to start on the paper where the previous cut was finished.

The Paper Saver button automatically reorders your selection

Take up as little space as possible on your paper if you enable the paper saving function, it becomes your Default settings The paper key is backlit in green when active

Sharp characters

size choice

Use the size wheel to choose one of the sizes Settings between 0.25 inches (0.64 cm) and 23.5 inches(59.69 cm). This determines the height of your finished the cut. The selected size is displayed on the screen next to the keyboard cover. Although the full-size range is available Be sure, regardless of the size of the cutting mat Choose a size that fits your material use.

The term machine has four measurement units: inches - 1/4, inches - 1/10, cm and mm. In the Settings menu, select the desired unit of measurement

Cut off your selection

Press the CUT button.

The STOP button is located next to the CUT

This key stops the current process.

When the Cricut Expression Engine is finished

Cut out, press the Unload paper button on

Keyboard for ejecting the cutting mat and the paper

the machine.

Remove your characters from the cutting mat.

Carefully remove the images from the cutting mat. If that

is difficult to remove characters, use a craft

Knife or the Cricut Tools ™ (sold separately) for

lift the pictures carefully. Once all the characters are

Remove any small pieces of paper

stay on the cutting mat. That will improve

Performance of cutting mats in the future.

Shadow function

Shadow is the most commonly used creative feature of the Cricut ™ font.

And shape the cartridges. Selecting this option creates a proportionally larger size.

Shaded image of each selected character. When the shadow function is active. The shadow button is backlit in green. The length adjustment mode allows you to adjust the size the length of a particular section. This mode is only available in landscape format. The mode eliminates the uncertainties of the setting of The height of each cut with the size dial and hoping to cut a certain length. Use Adjust the length and press the Adjust Length Button, so that the button is backlit green.

Then you decide on the cut the length with the size wheel on the right side from the front of the machine. Press CUT and the display shows a preview of the height before the machine starts cutting. The length mode is adjusted applies to all cuts on the screen.

The auto-fill mode fills the page with so many selected characters on the screen stand on the page in the chosen size. To the Auto Fill, press the AutoFill button to make sure The button is backlit in green. So do your Character selection (s), set the size wheel and press CUT.

Settings

On the Settings screen, you can change the language, units of measure, Cutting parameters, carpet size, and representation of the character images. The screen settings are determined

the machine settings, which are the default values each time the machine is used. To access the settings screen, press the Settings button until it is green backlit

The display shows the first setting menu. There are five preference menus:

1. In the Language menu, you can select one of the following four languages: English, French,

Spanish or German) for on-screen instructions and information.

2. In the Units menu, you can select one of the four measurement units (inches -

1/4 inch - 1/10 cm or mm).

3. In the Multiple Cuts menu, you can select the number of cuts to use (2, 3 or 4).

For the multi-cut mode.

4. In the standard carpet size menu, you can choose the size of the carpet (12 "x 12" or 12 "x 24").

You will cut with it.

5. Use the Character Images menu to select whether preview images should be displayed

Display or display of thumbnails on display (Do not show).

Use the left and right arrow keys to scroll through the various options.

And the OK button is used to make a selection. Press the OK button to advance to the next menu and press the SETTINGS button to exit.

Mat Size

The Mat Size button is a quick way to set the mat size that you will be using with

the Cricut Expression machine. Load the mat and then press the button to change

to 12" by 12" or 12" by 24". The default mat size can also be changed on the

Settings screen.

Extra Buttons

The Xtra1 and Xtra2 buttons are placeholders for future functions for the Cricut Expression™ machine.

Sizing

Characters in the Cricut cutting system are measured from the lowest possible point to the highest possible point. In font sets and some shape sets, the character shown in red is the Key Height Character. This is usually the tallest character in any one set. All

other characters will be sized in proportion to the Key Height Character unless Real Dial Size is selected. In shape sets, some images are also cut in proportion to other shapes. See the cartridge handbook to get the details on specific cuts.

Frequently asked Questions

Q: Do I have to hold down the Shift key to use it?

A: No, just press once, and the backlight will turn green to indicate that it is being used.

Q: Are the creative function keys the same for each cartridge?

A: For most sets, only the shadow feature is available. The other five creative features are

selected and varied by the artist.

Q: How long does the blade last?

A: 500 to 1500 simple cuts, depending on the material

Cutting replacement blades are inexpensive and easy to change. Please refer

"Replacing the Cutting Blade" on page 21 of this manual.

Q: How long does a cutting mat last?

A: Depending on the size of the cuts, each rug keeps between 25 and 40 complete cuts.

And what kind of materials do you cut? We recommend the use of multiple carpets by turning them often. This will extend the life of each carpet.

Q: Can I use a paper size smaller than that of the cutting mat?

A: absolutely! Just align a smaller corner of the paper with the lower left corner of

the carpet, even in portrait mode. Once the carpet is loaded, use the Blade navigation menu.

Keys to move the cutting blade in the upper right corner of the new paper.

Then press the Set Keypad Format button to inform the device.

Where to cut the new paper size.

Q: Do I have to cut an entire page before unloading the cutting mat?

You can remove the paper and only remove the required parts. You can do that then

Reload the paper later and move the blade into an open area to continue cutting. If you are using the same paper for a new cut immediately, press the Load button.

Last key instead of the paper loading key. The Load button automatically returns the cutting blade to the point where it finished cutting.

Q: How does the paper saving mode work?

A: The Paper Saving mode "wraps" all selected cuts to maximize the required space.

Q: What is the actual size of the dial?

A: By default, your Cricut Expression ™ system cuts the characters proportionally. However, if you want to "break" that part and have all characters cut to the actual composition size, press the Current Size button. For example, with the parameter Size Dial

At 2 ", a small letter is cut 2.54 cm (1") to fit it in proportion to any other letter. If the actual size of the dial is selected, the same a should be cut to 5.08 cm (2 ").

Q: How is the cut off a character measured?

A: Each cut character is measured from the lowest possible point to the highest possible point.

CHAPTER 8: HOW TO START FIRST CUT

How To Cut Vinyl With A Cricut Machine: A Step By Step Guide

How to cut vinyl with a Cricut machine manual

Open your project or create a new one

First, open Cricut Design Space and create a new project or open a saved project. You can use images from the Cricut library, create a Make It Now project, or upload your image.

Prepare your project for the cut.

If you are performing a Make It Now project or using an image found in the Cricut Image Library, you may be able to skip the following steps. These images are usually all ready to go without additional effort directly to the machine.

If you've loaded your image (in JPEG or SVG format), here are some simple tips on managing layers, colors, and groups to prepare the image for editing.

You can check if your image is ready for editing by clicking on the green "Make It" button in the upper right corner.

If the following screen displays your image, separated by colors or layers, with the appropriate spacing and orientation, you can start! Ignore the rest of this section and send your image to the machine for cutting.

However, if the following forms screen appears colored but not correctly spaced, you must click the gray Cancel button to go back and make some adjustments before sending the drawing to your Cricut. get cut

To maintain the correct spacing of your image, forms must be "appended" to Cricut Design Space. Start by selecting all shapes of color (in this case all red bands) by holding down the Shift key and clicking each red band in the image. You can also hold down the Shift key and right-click on each red stripe layer in the Layers panel.

When you have selected all the colors, click the gray Attach icon in the lower right corner of the Layers panel. When you combine layers, group them so that they shift as you move or resize the image. This also causes the layers to be aligned exactly as they appear on the screen when you cut, rather than treating them as a group of individual shapes that can be rotated or moved.

Repeat this process for all other "groups" of shapes that are properly spaced (in this case the white stripes).

Send your picture to the machine to cut it.

When all your different colors are attached, click the green Create button to send the image to cut on your computer.

Their design is automatically divided into different carpets depending on the color. In this way, you can create a multicolored or multi-layered design in a project!

Edit the Project Copies box to make multiple copies of your project. Then set the material size for each rug. When cutting a fusible vinyl, make sure you change the mirror switch. You can also move the images to the right in the preview of the carpet if you like.

If everything is ok, click on the green "Next" button.

From there you can just follow the instructions on the screen! Make sure your Cricut computer is turned on and displayed in the Connect Machine window at the top of the screen. Put the device's Smart Dial on vinyl (or if you have an old device without a smartphone)

Glue a piece of vinyl over your cutting mat to make sure the back of the paper is facing down.

Then load the carpet into your Cricut machine by pressing the flashing load / unload button.

Load the cutting mat into the Cricut machine to cut the vinyl

Once the carpet is loaded, you will be prompted to press the flashing start button.

Cut the vinyl with the Cricut machine in several layers or colors.

The display will show a progress bar while your machine finishes the cut. When the cut is complete, the screen prompts you to press the Load / Unload button to unload the cutting mat.

Load the second vinyl color into the Cricut machine to cut the vinyl in several colors

If you only have one color, it's over!

If you want to cut a second or third color, gently remove the vinyl from the cutting mat and place the next vinyl paint on the mat. Load the cutting mat into the machine by pressing the load / unload button and then press the start button when it starts to flash. Repeat this process until all carpets are cut.

When the final cut is complete, unload the cutting mat and click the green Finish button on your screen to return to your project. And you are done!

You can now remove the background vinyl and apply it to your project! Here's an excellent tutorial on applying vinyl with transfer paper. She cut her project out with her Silhouette machine, but the transfer paper part is the same, no matter which machine your design is cut with.

CHAPTER 9: SOLVING THE MOST COMMON PROBLEM WHEN USING CRICUT

What is a Cricut maker?

Cricut Maker is an intelligent cutting machine that works in conjunction with printers. To use this, create patterns on your computer and then print them on the device as you would on a traditional printer. However, Cricut Maker does not just print the design: it cuts it off from the material you specify, such as paper, craft foam, paper, fabric, vinyl and imitation leather.

With Cricut Maker, you can do many projects, including:

Letters and funny shapes for scrapbooking

Onesie and shirt design

Custom cards

leather Bracelets

Masks for painting

Party favors

Vinyl stickers for cars

Monogram Pillow

Christmas decorations

Designs for tumblers, mugs, and cups

wall Stickers

wood signs

Decals for home appliances

How to install Cricut Maker

To install Cricut Maker on your Mac, follow these steps:

Connect the Cricut Maker to a power source and turn it on.

Connect it to your Mac via Bluetooth.

Download and install the Cricut Design Space App for Mac.

After installation, open the application and follow the instructions on the screen to create a Cricut ID.

If you have an account, go to the menu area and touch Machine Setup and App Layout.

Choose New Machine Configuration.

Complete the setup by following the instructions on the screen.

If you are already being asked to create your first project, the configuration is successful and complete.

To solve the problems of Cricut Maker

Design Space, the developers of Cricut Maker, are aware that their product has problems, including slow loading, outages, and blocking. For this reason, they constantly update the application and the design of the machine.

In the meantime, these are the possible solutions to the reported problems.

1. Correct your internet connection.

The main reason that Cricut Maker machines have problems is a slow internet connection. The Cricut Design Space app requires fast, stable upload and download speeds to send and receive information while working on a drawing. If the connection is inconsistent, the application may hang or freeze.

According to Design Space, the application requires a download speed of at least 2 Mbps and a download speed of 3 Mbps to work effectively. If your Internet speed is not at the same level, contact your Internet service provider. They can provide you with a new modem or update your Internet plan to reach the required speeds.

2. Check the specifications of your computer.

If this is not your Internet speed, the problem may be with the specifications of your Mac. To run the Cricut Maker Design Space application, certain minimum requirements must be met. Here you are:

For Windows computers:

Windows 8 or higher

Intel Core or AMD processors

4 GB RAM

500 MB of available hard disk space

Bluetooth connection

For Apple computers:

Mac OS X 10.12 or higher

83 GHz CPU

4 GB RAM

50 MB of available hard disk space

Bluetooth connection

3. Close any unneeded background programs.

Another possible reason why Cricut Design Space is not loaded is the fact that many programs are running in the background. This is usually the case when you watch Netflix, skype with your friends, or upload your current vlog to YouTube.

Well, the accessories should be multitasking for you. However, if you want to use Cricut Design Space, you can close applications and tabs that you do not need. You will see how it will speed things up!

In addition to closing unneeded applications and programs, you may also want to do the following:

Clear the cache and history of your browser.

Perform a quick scan with Outbyte MacRepair to remove unwanted files.

Run a full malware scan.

4. Refresh your browser and clear the cache.

Your browser can prevent you from running Cricut Maker Design Space. For the application to work, you need to run the latest version of your browser. Whether you're using Firefox, Chrome or Safari, make sure it's updated.

After updating your browser, delete its history, cookies, and cache. Then close the browser and restart it from the desktop. Run the Cricut Maker application again.

5. Do not perform test cuts

To avoid waste of material, it is best to perform one or more small test sections each time you insert the blade holder and cut a new material. Do not assume that the recommended settings for a particular material are always accurate. Many factors affect the way a material is cut, including the sharpness of the blade, the condition of the carpet, the complexity of the design, the effect of moisture, and the color of the dye used in the material. If you can not do a good test, trust me, the rest of your project will also be unsuccessful. It's also a good idea to choose a form similar to the one used in your project. In other words:

-When you cut a title, use a small letter as the cut shape.

- When cutting a rhinestone pattern, test a small pattern with, say, ten circles of similar size to those used in rhinestone design.

- When you cut large, simple shapes, you can use a basic shape such as a circle, a square, or a heart.

6. Discard bad cuts on bad factors

The most extreme example of "blame for the wrong thing" is when customers reinstall the software to try to "fix a bad cut." This is not a solution to a cutting problem! This can be the solution if the computer and the cutting tool are not communicating well. In this case, a reinstallation of the driver should be tried first.

Discover the possible causes of various problems, such as:

Nothing cuts itself off - the power is too weak; not enough exposure of the blade; the blade is too high above the material; The blade is struck

- partial cuts - the strength is too weak; the blade is too close to the material; the material is not stabilized; more than one passage is necessary; The speed is too high

- Wear - too much exposure of the blade; the strength is too high; The material was exposed to moisture. The material is not suitable for cutting

-The end point is offset from the starting point - The force is too high (weaker force and more passes required); the speed is too high; the material is not stabilized; The underside of the carpet is sticky

-Changes and rounded corners - the offset of the blade is too weak

- Bubbles in the outer corners and depressions in the inner corners - the offset of the blade are too large

7. Not fully stabilizing the material for cutting

Stabilization is the process of having on the material a kind of support that is not penetrated by the blade. This support prevents the material from moving through the blade and prevents the cut parts from falling out of the material while other parts of the project continue to be cut. Vinyl and many heat-sealable products already have a backing layer that is not penetrated by the blade and serves as a stabilizer. However, paper products must be stabilized by pressing on a clean and sticky carpet that is not allowed to be penetrated by the blade but only scratched by the tip.

If someone with a problem is in a place where there are no clean cuts (see photo above), I'll ask him first to closely check the cutting mat to see if the performance is true sticky lack of these places. This often happens right where the pinch rollers run over the carpet. However, it may simply be a general loss of adhesiveness due to the accumulation and interference of invisible material fibers.

The cutting mats can be washed with warm water and some soap. Through this process, these fibers can be absorbed by water and washed away. The glue still on the carpet will not be removed and after drying the surface should become very sticky again. However, check the entire surface and add more non-repositionable adhesive to places that no longer stick. You can also use a Goo Gone or Duck Adhesive Remover to completely remove a carpet and then apply a new thin film.

8. Leave too much blade on the blade holder

For the first time, the problem with the Wishblade and Craft Robot cutters ten years ago was a catchy problem. Users could not understand why increasing blade exposure (by changing the color of the cap on these blade holders) did not solve the incision problems that had occurred. The fact remains the same with all knives: A larger blade does not lead to a better cut. The displayed blade quantity should match the material thickness and the minimum possible amount. If you have many more exposed blades, not only will you cut off the carpet unnecessarily and release the blade, but you will see more drops of tears, crumpled corners, and incomplete cuts. If the end of the blade protrudes into the carpet and is raised at the end of a path, the material is more likely to be separated from the carpet and destabilized and eventually ruptured.

9. Assuming a blade is chipped

The blades may be machinable when the blade holder is dropped onto a hard surface. On machines with high forces, a blade can be hit with too big a blade, even if it is too heavy. The blade not only penetrates the material but is pushed into the carpet, hitting the hard surface. That is, chips are not very common and should not be taken into account if you suddenly get incomplete cuts. On the one hand, most shredded blades cut no material at all, as opposed to a less perfect cut.

The best way to determine if the blade has flaked off is to scan, as a scanner magnifies the image, which greatly facilitates the inspection of the blade tip. Some blades now have a reduction to reduce offset size and allow smaller details. Do not confuse the reduction as a broken blade.

10. Not understanding what blade offset does and does not do

Sometimes the blade misalignment is mistakenly blamed for cutting problems. At other times, the cause of rounded corners, bubbling corners, or hanging panes is completely forgotten (cuts that are barely associated with the debris on which the blade starts and stops). So take the time to understand what this parameter does. Note that for knives with a limited range of knives, the setting is built into the firmware. However, if you find this parameter in your cutting software, it is important that you understand it.

Blade offset is a correction where the tip of the blade is at a slightly different location than the center of the blade shaft.

CHAPTER 10: TIPS AND TRICK TO MAKE CRICUT EASIER AND EFFICIENT

CRICUT TIPS AND TRICKS FOR BETTER, EASIER CRAFTING

Cricut is ready to go, but can do a lot more! Here are some Cricut tips and tricks to help you get the most out of this amazing machine.

CUTTING WITH YOUR CRICUT

If your material does not adhere well to the carpet, stick it with blue tape or masking tape.

If you have a project that needs to be cut on two different materials (e.g. green box and red box), you can cut at the same time. Simply place the patterns to be cut in different areas of the canvas in Cricut Design Space, select everything, click Append, and place your materials in the same places on your carpet.

Always test your waste before using your expensive, stylish and unique equipment. This will save you money and a headache!

If you cut a particularly difficult or thick material, your Cricut will probably cut it several times. What happens if that is not enough? Cut again Hold the mat in place (do not press the arrow button to eject it) and press the "C" (Go) button again. She is cut again.

PRINT AND CUT

Use an inkjet printer when printing and cutting. It seems to work much better than a laser printer. The calibration light used in the meter to read the marks can heat the toner and prevent it from reading. I'm using an HP inkjet printer that's great for printing and cutting.

Cricut probably can not read the registration marks if you want to print and cut on white paper. So print the labels on white paper, cut them out, and stick them on your non-white paper before you put them in your Cricut! Or, cut these registration marks on sticker paper and place them over the markings on your colored paper.

If you want to use the maximum size of the image with the Print & Cut feature, use the Chrome, Safari, or Internet Explorer browsers, which can display images up to 6,75 inches (6.75 cm) wide.

WRITE WITH YOUR CRICUT

Do you like to write with Cricut pens, but do not like the costs? Try out Round Stic Bic Pens, Crayola Fine-Line Markers, Gelly Roll Metallized Gel Pens or American Craft Slick Engravers.

Are you having trouble putting your non-Cricut pen in the right position for writing? When inserting the pen, place a pen under the clip A and stop it when kissing the pen. Close the clamp, take out your stick, and your pen is in the ideal position.

If you want to use another pen that is too thin, try sticking the body until it is tight.

Put the cap of your pen in your built-in accessory bucket. So your ink stays near the top and is ready to use!

RATING WITH YOUR CRICUT

You can purchase a separate marker pen and place it in the pen holder to record the documents. The notation generally facilitates the folding.

When you create your designs, you can double the result line on your canvas for better and deeper results.

EMBOSSING WITH YOUR CRICUT

If you want to use your Cricut for embossing, get an accessory adapter, replace the blade case with this adapter, insert your incisor pin and ask the Cricut Design Space to cut. It will shape instead! You get better results if you put something with a small gift under the material you want to emboss.

BLADES FOR YOUR CRICUT

Use a different blade to cut the paper than you cut the vinyl. This extends the life of the blade and allows for sharper cuts. Color code for your blades by painting the tip of the plastic blade cover with acrylic paint - white for paper, black for vinyl, etc.

If your blade does not cut so well, paint a foil of aluminum foil over your carpet and cut out a simple pattern. This helps sharpen your blade a bit. I do that, and it works.

DESIGNING FOR YOUR CRICUT

Cricut Design Space offers free weekly drawings! Note that they are free for this week only. However, if you save them in a project and try to use them after the free week, you may have to pay for them. Use it or lose it!

You should not only use the fonts on your system or in Cricut Design Space. You can download new fonts, install them on your computer, and get access.

Remember to install dingbat and glyph fonts for easy access to images and icons!

You can upload your files to Cricut Design Space. The system accepts SVG, DXF, JPG, BMP, GIF and PNG files. However, SVG and DXF work better because they are vector-based. If SVG or DXF is not an option, use PNG to get the best quality. If you do not know how to search and download SVG files

Pay attention to the order of levels in Cricut Design Space, as your Cricut first cuts and leaves the lower level. So it's a good idea to place the big outlines as the top layer to be last edited to prevent your material from slicing and slipping as your Cricut cuts out the small details.

CRICUT MATS

If you want to remove the finished project from the carpet, turn it down and peel it off of the material instead of trying to remove it. This will prevent your equipment from buckling during the removal process.

Keeping carpets clean is difficult, especially if you live in a house with pets. Keep a lint near your Cricut and use it after each application on your carpet. Then place the protective film back on the sticky side of the mat to prevent dust from falling on it.

If your carpet is no longer sticky, wash it with mild detergent in warm water. I like to rub detergent (without lotion) in a circular motion all over the carpet until it is covered. Rinse and air dry.

Another remedy for the stick is to rub a Lysol / Clorox Bleach cloth or baby cloth on the surface.

If you accidentally cut your mat, secure it with tape or gorilla tape on the back of the mat.

If you repeat the same cut over and over again and wear a cut path in your carpet, turn it and use the other side to get the wear.

If you need to buy new carpets, you can save money by cutting the 12 x 24-inch rugs in half to cut them in half to 12 x 12 inches.

MATERIALS

Buy your record at a location other than your local craft store at the best prices.

Do you not need a specific color of the map material? Try to print this exact color on a white piece of cardboard before cutting it. The same can be done with vinyl with spray paint!

Use clear contact paper instead of expensive transfer sheets to remove the vinyl from the paper support. I think it works better too!

Are you tired of your vinyl rolls loosening and unfolding? Use paper rolls or toilet paper rolls - just cut a long slot in the box and place it on your vinyl roll.

WEEDING

It can be difficult to get these tiny pieces of paper or vinyl from a drawing. Try a safety pin for very small things.

Dip your weeding tool into something sticky and use it to pick up the pieces faster.

Store your weeding tool and all other cute Cricut tools on a breadboard near your machine. Here is my Cricut tool holder made from an old frame and some perforated plates:

ASSEMBLY OF PROJECTS

I'm a big fan of Aleene's Tacky glue, which allowed me to put together my projects when I wanted a little margin for positioning. But it takes time to dry. If you want a faster adhesive, try Beacon Adhesives Zip Dry Paper Adhesive. It is an adhesive that dries faster and is very sticky!

CHAPTER 11: BEGINNERS PROJECT TO START USING CRICUT MACHINE

CRICUT PROJECTS FOR BEGINNERS

1. STICKERS

HOW TO MAKE STICKER WITH CRICUT PRINT THEN CUT

Provisions:

Cricut Explore Air ™ 2 machine

Cricut Printable Sticker Paper

Step 1. Log in to Cricut Design Space to start creating! If you do not have an account yet, you only need one minute to create an account.

Step 2. Start a new project in Cricut Design Space, then click on the left side of the screen and specify "Images." Use the search bar at the top right of the screen to search for images you like, such as Ice cream.

Step 3. Click each ice cream and click the Flatten button in the lower right corner of the screen. This will turn every ice cream into a piece, rather than a separate file for each piece of ice.

Step 4. Resize each ice by clicking on it and then dragging the right side of the box to the desired size. I made each ice about 1 ", so it fits well with my spoons and my cups of ice cream.

Step 5. Your drawing is ready for printing. Click "Save" in the upper left corner to save your project and save it as "Print" and then "Cut." Click the large green Make It button in the upper right corner of the screen.

Make sure everything is OK and click Next. You will be prompted to print the drawing on paper (be sure to insert sticker paper when making labels).

Step 6. When your drawing is printed, set the dial on your Cricut Explore Air ™ 2 to the correct setting, if you are using thick Cricut sticker paper, use the "Vinyl" setting.

Place your sticker paper on the cutting mat and place it in the machine by pressing it against the rollers. Press the flashing button "Load/Unload."

Press the flashing "Go" button to cut your stickers. These stickers are small and complex, so it takes a few minutes to cut them.

2. CHRISTMAS TEA TOWELS

EASY CHRISTMAS TEA TOWELS WITH CRICUT EXPLORE AIR

Christmas tea towels are a quick and easy project for beginners with the Cricut Explore Air cutting machine! Just add a heat transfer vinyl, and your design options are virtually unlimited!

First, open the Cricut design area and start a new project. The Cricut Design Space image library contains more than 60,000 images to choose from. It's easy to design your project in no time! Just click on the image you want to work with, and the software will paste it into a new project document. I've selected these beautiful "Merry Christmas" and "Merry and Bright" designs for the dishcloths with letters in my hand and included them in the project document to match my sheet of heat transfer vinyl.

Set the knob to "iron," and you can cut Cricut Explore Air

Place a heat transfer vinyl film on the cutting mat (glossy side down), place it in the machine, press the cut-off button and place the vinyl wrap on my carefully folded towel. Then cover 'a piece of cloth (actually another cloth!) And ironed according to the instructions on the package.

Once the heat transfer film firmly adheres to the fabric, remove the plastic backing and discard it.

Slide a piece of cardboard under the top of the towel and use gold, silver and champagne metallic paint to add light spots. Allow the paint to dry completely before removing the underlying protective layer!

3. DIY LEATHER KEY FOB

DIY LEATHER KEY FOB GIFT IDEA WITH CRICUT

Provisions:

Keychain templates

Cricut explore air 2

Cutting mat with standard handle

Grained artificial leather sample pack (I used black and blue colors)

Imitation leather - silver, brown and beige

Black pencils by Cricut (optional for customization)

Paper craft set

Clear Gorilla glue

rivet

key ring

Procedure:

Open keychain models in Cricut Design Space DIY.

Choose your pattern and set the Cricut Wheel to Custom. Then choose artificial leather. If you want to customize your DIY leather keychain, also load a Cricut pen into the machine and hit Go.

Note: Although there are three different styles, most instructions for DIY leather keychains apply to all.

Poke holes where the rivet will get Using the Piercer from the paper crafting set. Make the hole large enough for the base of the rivet to penetrate, but it should be well set up.

Slide the key ring onto the keyring. Slide the long end of the rivet from the back of the key ring through all layers. Place the top of the rivet on the base of the rivet, place the hammer directly on the rivet and beat the cylinder.

4. DIY HOME DECOR

SIMPLY DIY HOME DECOR | MAKING A PERSONALIZED PILLOW WITH CRICUT

What you need:

Cricut Maker or your favorite Cricut Machine

Glitter Iron-On Vinyl (or vinyl of your choice)

Cricut EasyPress

EasyPress Mat

Iron the protective foil

Pillowcase and insert of your choice

Step 1 - Open Cricut Design Space on your smartphone. On the Home tab, click New Project.

Step 2 - Then select the text icon at the bottom of the screen and select the desired font. Enter your last name and drag the corner of the field to zoom in or out according to your size.

Step 3 - Then select the text icon again to insert the second line of text for your east. Year. Drag to the right size and center it under your last name

Step 4 - Then select the two text boxes at once and click the Attach button. It is displayed when you click the Actions button. This connects the two text boxes so that they are centered.

Step 5 - Then click the "Make It" button and the carpet screen will be displayed. Here you want to make sure that the mirror is "on."

Step 6 - To turn mirror setting on or off, click on the carpet image in the upper left corner. The screen above appears. Just activate the mirror button.

Step 7 - The rug now displays your mirror image, and you can load your Iron On Vinyl SHINY SIDE DOWN onto your rug. Click Next and follow the instructions!

Step 8 - When the pattern is cut, remove the excess vinyl and center the pattern on the pillowcase.

Step 9 - Then set the temperature and timer on EasyPress for your vinyl and shirt. Refer to the convenient EasyPress setup table.

Step 10 - Cover the pattern with the backing to be ironed, place EasyPress on the backing and press the Cricut button. Remove as soon as the timer has rung. Flip up your pillowcase and warm your back for 10-15 seconds.

Step 11 - Allow the iron to cool and simply remove the transfer sheet.

5. PERSONALIZED WATER BOTTLES

PROVISIONS

Bottle of water with a smooth surface

Vinyl outdoors

Transfer Tape

Scraper or brayer

This is such a simple project to make. Open the Cricut Design Space and design your text.Then create a second text field and make your start big! Tie the two layers together so that your name and your name are cut together, and adjust the size according to your water bottle. If you respect the bottle, start in the middle of your letter and practice. Smooth the bubbles as much as possible. Carefully remove your transfer ribbon, and you're done!

CHAPTER 12: FAQ

Cricut Maker FAQ

How does the Cricut machine work?

Cricut brings project ideas to your computer via Cricut Design Space and cuts, marks or draws the design on your material. What can be created is amazing, and the more projects you do, the more you think about it.

Is the design SPACE for the manufacturer Cricut the same as for the Explorer?

The design SPACE is indeed the same for the manufacturer Cricut as for the exploration. Use the

same URL for access and the same Cricut ID for the connection. However, during the editing interaction, if you select a Cricut Maker machine for the Set Material and Load options.

The tools and steps of the carpet will look a bit different with Cricut Maker have a Smart Set dial. The material is selected in the software instead.

Will I lose my cartridges, projects or uploaded images if I upgrade to Cricut Maker?

No. Your downloaded tapes, projects, and images are linked to your Cricut ID

Cricut Cloud, no machine. Always use the same Cricut ID

Access all your content with your Cricut Maker.

Is the Cricut Maker power cable the same as my Explore device?

The power cord of the Cricut Maker has been upgraded to allow a 3 amp output. the

Cricut Explore machines have a capacity of 2.5 amps. Increased capacity allows

allows charging a mobile device through the charging port on the right side of the Cricut

Machine while the machine is cutting or writing.

Using an Explore power cord with your Cricut Maker will not damage the device.

However, if you load a mobile device while the machine is cutting,

If you cut thicker materials or need more pressure, use something

A power cord other than the Cricut Maker power cord may cause the motor to stutter, slow it down,

or the extinguisher

How is the Cricut Maker Adaptive Tool System different?

The Cricut Explore Cut Smart technology moves the carpet back and forth into the machine and cart, allowing the thin blade to slide through Materials.

Cricut Maker also moves the carpet into the machine and cartbfrom side to side, but with the adaptive tooling system, the gears mesh with the adaptive tooling system to intelligently lift and turn the blade. Check the direction of the blade and the cutting pressure to reach the material.

Allow the rotating blade to cut tissue and the knife blade to cut thicker materials.

Does the Cricut Maker have a fast mode?

Yes; Cricut Maker offers a fast mode option for cutting and writing up to 2x faster with some vinyl, iron and cardboard settings

How does the manufacturer Cricut know which blade I have Loaded?

When you cut your project, the machine first moves the carriage to

on the right side (call "Homing"), then scan the blade for the installed one.

Should the Cricut Maker be connected to the internet?

The Cricut Maker is used with Design Space, a cloud-based online solution Software. It does not work alone. When using Design Space on a desktop Or a laptop requires an internet connection. When using the machine with You can use the offline feature with the Space app on an iOS device (iPad / iPhone).

In this app, you can use your machine and your design SPACE without an internet connection

Is it easy to download my images with Cricut?

It is easy enough. The simpler the design, the easier or faster it can be downloaded.

Is there an evaluation tool for the Cricut Expression?

There is a scoreboard with a case that you can use with the expression machine. Just swap it with your Expression Blade case and write down your project.

What materials can a Cricut Expression® machine cut?

Cricut Expression can cut a variety of materials, including cardboard, vinyl, vellum, fabrics, chipboard, and even thin sheets.

What does the box contain with the Cricut Create machine?

Cricut Create Machine

User Guide

Don Juan cartridge, cartridge belt, keyboard, and handbook

Blade assembly

One 6"x12" (15.24 cm x 30.48 cm) cutting mat

Quick Start Guide

Power adapter.

CONCLUSION

Cricut Machines simplifies all projects and tasks related to cutting, tracking and precision manufacturing. Cricut Machines gives you the freedom to create any kind of project, from paper craft to vinyl decals. Simply connect your tablet, smartphone or computer to a Cricut computer to get your project up and to run.

There are various Cricut models to choose from. If you're considering buying a Cricut for your home or business.

CPSIA information can be obtained
at www.ICGtesting.com
Printed in the USA
LVHW062050080621
689681LV00020B/2009